Feature and Narrative Storytelling for Multimedia Journalists

W9-DIJ-015

Feature and Narrative Storytelling for Multimedia Journalists

Duy Linh Tu

NEW YORK AND LONDON

DiPietro Library
Franklin Pierce University
Rindge, NH 03461

First published 2015
by Focal Press
70 Blanchard Road, Suite 402, Burlington, MA 01803

and by Focal Press
2 Park Square, Milton Park, Abingdon, Oxon OX14 4RN

Focal Press is an imprint of the Taylor & Francis Group, an informa business

© 2015 Taylor & Francis

The right of Duy Linh Tu to be identified as author of this work has been asserted by him in accordance with sections 77 and 78 of the Copyright, Designs and Patents Act 1988.

All rights reserved. No part of this book may be reprinted or reproduced or utilised in any form or by any electronic, mechanical, or other means, now known or hereafter invented, including photocopying and recording, or in any information storage or retrieval system, without permission in writing from the publishers.

Notices
Knowledge and best practice in this field are constantly changing. As new research and experience broaden our understanding, changes in research methods, professional practices, or medical treatment may become necessary.

Practitioners and researchers must always rely on their own experience and knowledge in evaluating and using any information, methods, compounds, or experiments described herein. In using such information or methods they should be mindful of their own safety and the safety of others, including parties for whom they have a professional responsibility.

Product or corporate names may be trademarks or registered trademarks, and are used only for identification and explanation without intent to infringe.

Library of Congress Cataloging-in-Publication Data
Tu, Duy Linh.
  Feature and narrative storytelling for multimedia journalists / Duy Linh Tu.
    pages cm
  1. Video journalism. 2. Digital video. 3. Online journalism. 4. Broadcast journalism. 5. Journalism—Authorship. 6. Journalism—Technological innovations. I. Title.
  PN4784.V54T83 2015
   070.4′9—dc23
   2014031705

ISBN: 978-0-415-72908-6 (pbk)
ISBN: 978-0-415-72907-9 (hbk)
ISBN: 978-1-315-85129-7 (ebk)

Typeset in Giovanni
By Apex CoVantage, LLC

SFI Certified Sourcing
www.sfiprogram.org
SFI-00453

Printed and bound in the United States of America
by Edwards Brothers Malloy

For Nicole, Lela, and Zoe.

For more information please visit my companion website: www.duylinhtu.com/edu

Contents

Acknowledgments

This book would not have been possible without the generous support and guidance of many fine people. First, I would like to give special thanks to my wonderful and incredibly understanding wife, Nicole. Without her, I never would have been able to travel, report, shoot, edit, teach, or learn any of the things that I cover in this book. She is my everything. Thank you to my two girls, Lela and Zoe. You angels always inspire dad to work harder and to tell better stories. Thanks to Thi Thi because she is simply the best mom ever. Thank you to my sisters, Ai Linh and Thuy Linh, for always looking out for me, then and now. Gracias a Abbey Adkison y Los Gorditos. Thanks to my talented colleagues at the Columbia Graduate School of Journalism, especially David Klatell, who taught me to shoot my first frame of video. Thanks to all the video journalists I've had the luck of meeting. Everything I know about this craft, I learned by watching you. And, finally, thanks to my editor, Katy. Your patience and wisdom made this coffee-shop idea into a reality.

PART

I

Modern Multimedia Journalism

CHAPTER 1

The State of Video

Much of the Midwest was still frozen from the Polar Vortex of 2013 when my colleague Abbey Adkison and I pulled into a parking garage a few blocks from the *Chicago Sun-Times* building. We were 4 months into researching and reporting our *Video Now* project, a study about the current state of video journalism in the United States (videonow.towcenter.org). The *Sun-Times* was one of our final stops on a long tour of newsrooms across the country. We had already visited places such as the *Detroit Free Press*, *The Seattle Times*, *Frontline*, and Mashable—a diverse selection of newspapers, digital properties, and documentary producers—to see how these organizations were staffing their teams, what kinds of videos they were producing, and how they were attempting to make money from news video.

We were particularly interested in visiting the *Chicago Sun-Times*. The paper had notoriously fired its entire photography staff in May 2013. At the time, management of the paper issued a statement hinting at future investments in video journalism.

"The *Sun-Times* business is changing rapidly and our audiences are consistently seeking more video content with their news," the paper said in the press release. "We have made great progress in meeting this demand and are focused on bolstering our reporting capabilities with video and other multimedia elements. The *Chicago Sun-Times* continues to evolve with our digitally savvy customers, and as a result, we have had to restructure the way we manage multimedia, including photography, across the network."

The layoffs had set off a wave of anger and disbelief from journalists and the public, especially on social media. But, for most in the journalism business, this move seemed inevitable. Newspapers, having had suffered a decade of massive job losses and shrinking advertising revenue, now needed a new stream of income. Video was one hope. In 2013, a typical banner ad on a news Web site could earn the publication one or two dollars per one thousand views. But a 15- or 30-second video pre-roll ad could make twenty or thirty times that much.

By the time we arrived at their offices on N. Orleans Street, the *Sun-Times* had already hired Dustin Park as Executive Producer in charge of video and

Figure 1.1

How is video produced today? The Tow Center's Video Now *report can be viewed at videonow. towcenter.org.*

a three-person team of video producers. Dustin is young, as are the other members of his production team. They are all in their twenties or thirties, an important fact to consider when discussing how and what kinds of news videos are made. While Dustin and his team grew up watching news on local or network TV, they now consume most of their videos online. And video online is nothing like the evening news on TV.

"It is always rolling around in my head. Where is the next frontier for documentary film? And where's the next frontier for documentary TV?" Dustin told us.

"I really strongly believe that's online. The thing that's even more liberating about online and encouraging and interesting is that you're not tied to a half-hour/

Figure 1.2

Executive Producer Dustin Park leads a new team of video journalists after the Sun-Times *management laid off its entire photo staff.*

hour model that is built into broadcast TV. You can produce a 5-minute, rich piece that's not going to take you months and months to do. But you can put a lot into that and make it look good and do great storytelling."

We spent two days in Chicago with Dustin, producers Peter Holderness and Jessica Koscielnia, and an intern. We observed their production processes and interviewed them and their bosses about video strategy. Like other newspapers we had visited in throughout the country, the *Sun-Times'* newsroom had been divided into two camps of video producers:

1. *Mobile Reporters.* Traditionally print-focused reporters had been outfitted with iPhones capable of shooting and uploading HD video from the field. These reporters contributed raw footage or lightly edited video pieces to go along with their text stories. Most importantly, the reporters uploaded these stories almost immediately from the field. They did not wait until the end of the day to publish.

2. *Video Producers.* Dustin's core team was focused on producing videos, and shot some photography. They produced packages, live shows, and several weekly sports, news, and political shows. These producers were experienced shooters and editors, and the content that they created, in most cases, had very high production value. Their stories tended to be more feature-length, and less breaking news in nature. These stories could take days or weeks to produce.

Figure 1.3
The iPhone has become a popular and powerful tool for producing news videos.

Figure 1.4
Sun-Times *videographers shoot a wide range of videos, including original in-studio shows.*

We saw a similar set up when we visited other newsrooms such as *The Seattle Times*, the *Detroit Free Press*, and the *Washington Post*. The newspaper industry, at least in 2014, seemed to be going with this two-prong approach: fast and mobile, or deep and highly produced.

Another observation we made during our research was that newspapers were very comfortable trying out various formats, ranging from raw video uploads to long-form documentaries. There is no time limit online and this has given editors a chance to play with style, length, and format.

"We do the raw clip. We do what I describe the uber clip, which is a little more fully formed package. Then we do the mid-sized, the 3- to 5-minute piece. And then we do the massive long-form stuff that is 45 minutes or a series. I think a video needs to be as long as a video needs to be to tell the story," said Kathy Kieliszewski, Director of Photo and Video at the *Detroit Free Press*.

WHO IS THIS BOOK FOR?

When I graduated from Columbia Journalism School in 1999 with a concentration in broadcast journalism, the news industry was much like it had been for many decades. There were four major TV networks, a few cable outlets, and the local news stations. At the time, the Internet was nearly non-existent in terms of producing news video.

A recent graduate like me, even from a respected program with a strong alumni network, had a long journey ahead before making it into the journalism

Big Leagues. I would have to work my way up from small TV markets in Iowa to mid-sized markets such as Milwaukee. Finally, after many years of hard work combined with a lot of luck, I might end up in a major market such as New York, L.A., or Chicago.

My job description as a broadcast journalist was just as well-defined as my career path. As a TV news producer, I found stories, directed camera operators to shoot, soundmen to record audio, and video editors to put my stories together in large, expensive AVID editing suites. There was even a driver to shuttle me around. At Columbia Journalism School, I had been taught to report, shoot, and edit my own stories. So, it was a shock when, at my first TV job, I had all these people working with me.

At the time, I was not overly concerned with the economics of the newsroom— the journalism industry was making a lot of money. Even so, it seemed strange to me that it took so many people to put together a 90-second story. Almost everything about the job of a video producer has changed since 1999.

Much has been written and discussed about the Internet and its disruptive effect on media, especially the business of journalism. News operations have shuttered bureaus, and newsrooms have seen their staffs cut in record numbers. According to the Poynter Institute, more than 18,000 editorial news jobs were cut from 2000 to 2012 (source: www.poynter.org/latest-news/business-news/the-biz-blog/216617/asne-census-finds-2600-newsroom-jobs-were-lost-in-2012/). News organizations have had to reconfigure their business and production models quickly, iterating strategies constantly. By the time this book is published, the industry will mostly likely have seen even greater challenges and changes come and go.

Another common topic of discussion in online newsrooms is the effect of this new age of journalism on the day-to-day life of a reporter. Journalists are being asked to do much more than ever before, with fewer resources. Those who have survived the many waves of layoffs are being retrained to blog and tweet, to take photos, and to produce video. There are no longer print-only reporters, nor are there massive video production teams, as there had been when I graduated from Columbia. A journalist, these days, works in several media and produces content that is published on several platforms.

This book and its accompanying Web site have been written and produced for the journalist and non-fiction storyteller of today, specifically those just starting to work with video. This text is designed for students, professional journalists looking to learn video production, or experienced producers looking to enhance their feature and narrative storytelling technique. This book will be also be useful for editors, professors, and others hoping to gain a better understanding of the processes and challenges of video production. This text can be read all the

Figure 1.5

Shooters at the Detroit Free Press must manage capturing both stills and video as a part of their jobs.

way through cover-to-cover, or readers may choose to jump to specific sections as needed. When possible, practice lessons and additional resources relating to material covered in the book have been made available online.

The structure of this book is based on the video curriculum that I have developed and taught at the Columbia Journalism School over the past decade. Many of the lessons and examples come from the courses that I still teach today. Throughout the book, I spotlight examples of excellent feature and narrative storytelling by multimedia journalists. In some cases, I have made available notes, raw material, and behind-the-scenes footage from my own projects.

Much of *Feature and Narrative Storytelling for Multimedia Journalists* is focused on skills development: production, shooting, audio recording, and editing. While I will demonstrate these techniques on specific hardware and software, this text is not about using any specific name-brand tools. You may use this book regardless of the make of your camera or the manufacturer of your editing software. However, I do advise that readers, if possible, shoot with large-sensor video cameras with manual exposure and audio controls. These cameras will provide greater flexibility and creative control in the field.

The second part of this book is focused on reporting and storytelling techniques. As Kathy Kieliszewski told me for the *Video Now* report: there are many ways to tell a story, and there are many forms of video. This text will focus on two specific types of video stories: video *features* (or shorter-form work) and *narratives* (longer documentaries). I also present information on the mobile video techniques used by journalists in modern newsrooms.

The bulk of this book is focused on high-end production of video stories, but it is vital that modern journalists also understand the importance of being able to produce in a Web-connected, mobile environment. I have also written this book with the assumption that many readers will be freelancers or independent journalists and I have dedicated a space towards social media, promotion, and distributing your projects online.

Whether you are a journalism student looking to produce high-quality video stories, a writer hoping to learn new skills, or a photographer looking to jump into video production, *Feature and Narrative Storytelling for Multimedia Journalists* has been written for you.

ORGANIZATION

This book has been organized into three main sections: defining modern multimedia journalism; principles of reporting, production, and post-production; and feature and narrative storytelling techniques. Also included in the book are detailed sections on social media and mobile production. The technical training program is based on my own experiences in the field and those of my colleagues. The reporting and storytelling sections are based directly on the video curriculum that I use at the Columbia Graduate School of Journalism. The mobile instruction portion of this book is based on the curriculum I developed to train working journalists through the journalism school's Continuing Education Program. The skills and techniques I cover in this text have been used personally, and have been taught to thousands of students for over a decade.

Figure 1.6
The Columbia University Graduate School of Journalism.

Hopefully, this textbook will give you the fundamental skills for producing high-quality video stories and documentary films. However, reading this book alone will not be enough to make you a great (or even competent) video storyteller. You must go out and practice—shoot daily and produce stories weekly. You must also network and find colleagues to work with and to learn from.

Throughout my career, I have been lucky enough to have met and work with some of the best video producers in the world. For this textbook, I asked some of the best editors, shooters, audio recordists, and editors in the field to give practical advice for new shooters and their answers are featured in each chapter. As you begin to produce your own work, build your network of trusted shooters, editors, colleagues, and friends. They will be your most valuable assets in the business.

The companion Web site of the book features additional editorial content, as well as video tutorials related to the chapters in the book. The Web site is often updated and can be used as a reference guide for years.

Q&A with the Experts: Kathy Kieliszewski, Director of Photography and Video, *Detroit Free Press*

How did you get started in video?
I made my first piece of "multimedia" in 1986 with an eight-track player, a cassette tape, a vinyl record and a bunch of still pictures cut out of teen magazines.

In my high school, we had a pretty extensive video production program and we were required to research, shoot, script, and edit packages that aired on the local cable access. Some were ok, most were not, but it helped propel me toward Michigan State University and the broadcast journalism department.

I switched over to still photography after my first year because there were so many prerequisite classes one needed to take before we got to grab a camera and go. I was antsy to start telling stories

Figure 1.7
Kathy Kieliszewski, Director of Photography and Video, Detroit Free Press.

since I had already done that in high school. So, I switched gears and followed the photojournalism track.

When the *Free Press* began producing video stories, I felt like I had come full
circle. My high school TV production teacher, Ms. Zappa, would have been
proud.

What kinds of stories work best for video?
Narrative stories with great characters, great visuals, and plenty of emotion,
moments, and surprises.

**What three tips would you give videographers in terms of finding and reporting
video-worthy stories?**
1. Find the focus. To use a newspaper term, what's the nut graf? Without
   a clear focus or nut graf, you don't have a story.
2. You can never have too many opportunities to gather b-roll.
3. Show, don't tell.

**How do you get someone to open up to you on camera? How do you get them
to "forget" that the camera is there?**
While setting up for the interview, just talk with a subject about everyday
things not necessarily related to the story. Distracting them with pleasant
chatter as you prepare for the interview and then transitioning into the interview naturally will loosen your subject up. Never say, "Ok, we are going to
start the interview now." Nothing will drain the color from a camera-shy person's face faster than that.

Sit eye-level with them, to the side of the camera, so that you can look at each
other. The more you treat this as a conversation and less like an interview, the
more likely the subject will be able to forget about the camera.

What are your best three interviewing tricks?
1. Don't ask questions. Have a conversation.
2. When you can, get your subject to show you rather than tell you.
3. Be quiet and listen.

What is in your gear bag? What gear does your team use at the Free Press**?**
- iPhone
- Canon 5D Mark III, Mark II or 6D
- Variety of lenses (preferably image stabilized)
- Rode shotgun mics
- Sennheiser shotgun mic
- Sennheiser wireless mic
- Headphones
- Tripod!
- We also have a Lite Panel kit for interviews, GoPros for fun stuff, sliders,
  and intervalometers for timelapses. Some of the photographers carry
  little beanbags for steadying their cameras without a tripod.

What kind of video works best for the Web?

It's all about content. A 45-second clip of something exclusive or emotional will do just as well as a 9-minute piece on people illegally parking in handicap parking spaces. I often use myself as a barometer for what I think will do well and subsequently, decide to commit resources to it. I literally have to think, "Damn, I'd watch that."

Knowing your audience is really key, too. Some things are universal: the turkey that chases a lady every time she tries to leave her house is Web video gold. Other things are very specific to your community. If you have a politician that everyone loves to hate, that may draw an audience. If you are taking people to the bottom of Lake Huron to see a never before seen shipwreck, you will draw an audience. If you have a large sports fan base, a sports columnist talking about draft picks or a new head coach might be a huge traffic driver.

The longer form documentary pieces have to be incredibly compelling, filled with rich characters, emotion, and a strong narrative to engage people for any length of time. Even with that, the success of that video depends on how actively it is promoted from the Web site and beyond.

What advice would you give to new video producers?

Learn the fundamentals of good audio, good interviewing, and most importantly, shoot for sequencing. Always shoot wides, mediums, tights, action/reaction, point-of-view so that in the edit you can take those individual shots and build scenes.

CHAPTER 2

The Elements of Video

THIS IS NOT TV

When I started my journalism career, the roles and job descriptions of journalists were clear. Writers wrote for newspapers and magazines, radio producers produced radio, and video people worked on local TV or at the networks. The concept of the multimedia journalist had not yet been born. These days, journalists are required to write, shoot photos, analyze data, create graphics, and produce video as regular functions of their jobs.

For as much as the job descriptions of journalists have changed, the style in which video content is produced at many publications has not. Only recently have papers such as the *Washington Post* begun to think of producing video specifically for a Web audience, rather than trying to mimic television-style reports. Digital-first companies like Vice have shown that online news videos can be very successful, if they are produced with an aesthetic and sensibility different than local TV news. Vice has nearly five million subscribers on YouTube, while most Web news videos get only hundreds or a few thousand views. So, how is Web video different than what we see on local TV newscasts?

The evening TV news was, and is, typically 30 minutes long, and about 8 of these minutes are reserved for commercials. This leaves just 22 minutes for TV reporters to give viewers the news of the day: politics, entertainment, business, sports, and, of course, weather. This premium on time has created the 90–120 second news story format, also called *packages*. It is rare to have a story go longer than a couple of minutes, and these stories have a style and form that have become so recognizable and cliché.

Online, there is no 30-minute show. Videos can be any length on the Web. This presents great opportunities for producers to tell *more* video stories, and to tell them in much greater depth. But the Web also brings with it big drawbacks and challenges for news organizations. In the past, ABC News was primarily concerned with its ratings against other networks such CBS and NBC.

Figure 2.1
Danny Gawloski of The Seattle Times *editing his long-form project, "Sea Change."*

Now, video producers are competing against social media, video games, apps, and big entertainment sites for their viewers' attention. Video producers must now present video stories that are compelling and unique enough to cut through the many distractions available online. Otherwise, their stories will be lost or buried.

Figuring out how to tell a Web-first video story has taken the journalism industry a lot of trial and error to figure out. I worked for an ill-fated dotcom in the early 2000s as a video producer. My online job was the same as it had been at the TV news network: I produced 60- to 90-second video packages that mimicked local TV news. That was over a decade ago, and it has only been within the past couple years that video producers have begun to change their style of storytelling: more cinematic videography, more in-depth character development, no standups from reporters, and no anchors back at the studio.

Today, the Internet has matured and the public's online news consumption habits have become distinct from what they are offline. People want news as fast or as in-depth as possible. Now, most news breaks or comes to us in the form of social media—on Twitter, Facebook, Instagram, or any other number of social platforms. By the time the local TV newscast starts at 6 PM, it is already hours behind the cycle. Online video producers must work at a much more accelerated schedule.

Another problem with following the local TV news format is that not all stories are best told in video form. Some stories should be 400 words. Some should be 140-character tweets. Some stories should be a single photo. Some should be data-driven multimedia extravaganzas. And, of course, some should be video. All these formats are possible online, but on TV, video is the only option. For decades, television producers have been forced to present all the news stories of the day, but they were not always using the best medium to tell these stories.

These days, video producers must produce fast, breaking news video or compelling in-depth video stories that provide more context or experience than print stories. This increases the chances that a reader will spend time watching and sharing the video online. The traditional TV news production cycle is neither fast enough to compete with Twitter (immediate, not at 6 PM), nor is it in-depth enough (only 90 seconds!) to compete with many of the documentary films appearing on the Web. This book will tackle how to produce these opposite modes of storytelling: mobile video, with its speed and immediacy; and narrative video, with its compelling and engaging story arcs. We begin with long-form.

VIDEO-WORTHINESS

What makes a story video-worthy? This is one of the fundamental questions video producers must ask themselves constantly. For many years, I had a difficult time clearly and concisely answering this question for my graduate students. I know a good video story when I see it, but what are the elements of that story that make it better told in video than in any other medium? At lunch one day, I asked my good friend and fellow professor Bob Sacha how he identified video-worthy stories.

"Motion and emotion," Bob said over a bowl of bibim bop at the Korean restaurant near my office. His answer was short and simple. And it is absolutely right.

Video works best when it features motion; it must demonstrate action in the camera (variety in shots and angles) and by the characters. Video does not work well when it is interview-based. The "talking head" video is often dull and tedious. Unless your sources are powerful politicians or popular celebrities, viewers will not want to watch them talk. They want to see videos with people in action. Chefs should be cooking, not talking about it. Athletes should be training or competing. Activists should be rallying their communities. Video stories should be active.

Video also succeeds when it conveys emotion—fear, rage, frustration, excitement, happiness, or hope—to the viewer. A family silently assessing the wreckage of their home after a hurricane makes for powerful footage. A toddler running

Figure 2.2a

A teacher is interviewed about using technology in education. This interview is important, but the shot is dull.

Figure 2.2b

An active shot of a teacher lecturing to his class.

to her father after he has returned from military service is compelling video. A team lifting their coach after a victory is a compelling scene. Videographers must look for opportunities to capture and demonstrate emotion in their videos.

If a story has either motion or emotion, then it is video-worthy. Ideally, a video story has both. If it has neither, it is most likely best told in another medium.

Unfortunately, many videos produced today do not feature enough motion or emotion. Many visual clichés, often called *wallpaper*, have developed over

Figure 2.3
Avoid shots that provide no editorial value. These images are often called "wallpaper."

time to approximate action. This generic type of video does not present new information, action, or emotion, nor does it advance the story. Local TV news video is plagued by wallpaper, shots of sources walking aimlessly down hallways, office workers typing at their keyboards, and scientists looking at beakers in unnamed laboratories. Even worse, video producers will also insert music into the stories to evoke mood, rather than finding the real emotion in their characters. While there is nothing inherently wrong with using music in your video stories, music should be used to enhance emotion, not create it.

TYPES OF VIDEOS

The Internet has opened up numerous opportunities for video producers to create and distribute their stories. Sites such as YouTube and Vimeo have provided video journalists with powerful distribution channels that can reach millions of potential viewers. These online platforms have also allowed for the production of video in forms and styles that were not possible before. Unlike TV, Web video goes well beyond the 90-second story. While it is too early to say what types of videos work best online, some forms have emerged to be very popular and successful on the Web.

Web video comes in many flavors:

1. *Traditional, broadcast-style videos.* Some newsrooms still mimic local TV-style reporting and production. TV networks with online properties

often repurpose their broadcast stories and repost these entire packages on the Web. These stories are not modified for a digital audience.

2. *Raw video.* Raw video clips are often shot and uploaded by print reporters using smartphones. Surveillance footage and user-generated content are used by news sites to enhance text stories.

3. *Explainer video.* Explainer videos tackle complicated topics such as health care reform or conflict in the Middle East. They typically feature motion graphics or an on-camera host explaining complex issues. These videos are usually only a few minutes in length. They are not traditional news stories or narratives, but they provide highly valuable news information.

4. *Interactive media.* Video can be integrated into rich multimedia presentations. For example, the *New York Times* and the *Guardian* both use video to enhance larger, complex projects. In these pieces, videos work jointly with other media and do not generally stand alone.

5. *Short feature videos.* Short feature videos typically feature interesting or newsworthy individuals or take a deeper look into specific topics. While these videos may have some news value, these are not breaking news stories. The shelf life of short features is much longer than that of breaking news stories. Viewers watch these videos months or years after their publication.

Figure 2.4

Traditional local TV-style video is not a popular form of video online.

Figure 2.5
Raw video can be uploaded quickly and can provide great news value for your audience.

Figure 2.6
News outlets such as the Washington Post *regularly produce animated explainer videos.*

6. *Documentary and long-form narratives.* Documentaries and long-form narrative videos are the most complicated and time-intensive stories to produce. These videos involve months of planning, shooting, and editing. Documentaries are expensive but often have great long-tail value—viewers will watch them long after their initial release and they can be distributed on multiple platforms such as Netflix or Roku.

Figure 2.7
The Seattle Times *produced "Sea Change," an in-depth multimedia project about ocean acidification.*

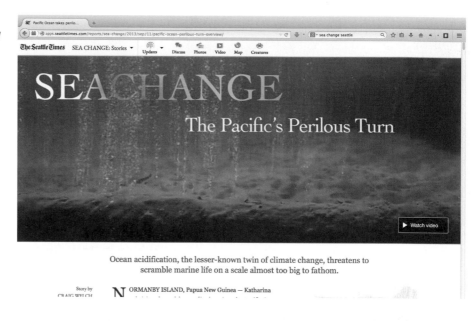

Figure 2.8
Kevin, the lead character from a film about children with deadly sun allergies, can only play outside when completely covered.

In the early days of the Web, the conventional wisdom of newsrooms was to keep video stories under 2 minutes. In the past few years, organizations such as Vice, *Frontline*, and MediaStorm have shown that online audiences have developed a big appetite for feature-length documentaries. Vice consistently gets millions of views for their films. Traditional news outlets such as the *New York Times* and *Time Magazine* have recognized the popularity of long-form video and have launched their own documentary divisions.

Figure 2.9
Josh, a main character from the film deepsouth, *sits in an abandoned building.*

In this book, we start off with feature and narrative storytelling techniques. We then move into mobile video. Although explainer videos are a powerful storytelling technique, they will not be covered in this text. Producing explainer videos requires a great understanding of design and animation that that is beyond the scope of this edition. We will be ignoring the techniques and style of TV news, a format that does not work well online.

Thinking Visually

One of the biggest challenges of becoming a video journalist is learning to *think visually*. What does this mean? A video producer must understand the components of video, and must be able to capture the elements needed to tell a compelling visual story. For print stories, reporting can be done in the field, on the telephone, or online. For video stories, all elements must be captured in the field, and video journalists must be able to identify the best visual components for the story. Video journalists need to identify and acquire interviews, *b-roll* or action, and natural sound efficiently and with careful attention to high production values.

Interviewing a source for a video story is very different than interviewing a source for print. There are production issues that you must be concerned about: lighting, location, environmental noise, and your sources' comfort and presence on camera. Casting the right characters for your video story and shooting them in the appropriate location are an important part of the production process.

There are also other editorial problems that video producers must solve, such as presenting scenes and events that occurred in the past. Often, videographers will have to illustrate or explain complicated statistics or other data. Videographers must constantly solve this fundamental question: How do I *visualize* my story?

As my colleague Bob Sacha said: video works when there is *motion* and *emotion*. Motion or action is often referred to as *b-roll*. Interviews and voiceovers are called a-roll. The roots of these terms go back many years to the early days of television when the news was shot on rolls of film. Video students and new video producers will often take this to mean that the a-roll is more important than the b-roll. That is, in fact, backwards.

The action of your story should be your main focus. Your interviews are undoubtedly important, but a-roll alone will only result in boring talking head videos. Understanding how to shoot *real* action and strong visual sequences is a major challenge and the primary goal of video production. As mentioned earlier, too many visual clichés have been established to replace real motion in TV news. Video journalists resort too quickly to using generic images in their stories. For example, local TV stories of crime will often feature generic images of poor urban areas. This is journalistically unsound, but also, the visuals give the viewer no true insight into the causes or solutions to crime.

Finding a story and reporting it thoroughly is the primary challenge of journalists in any medium. But for video journalists, finding a video-worthy story and reporting it takes a deep understanding of how visuals come together to tell a story. This can take years to master. The first step of learning how to produce video is understanding how to shoot authentic action and sequences.

Q&A with the Experts: Bob Sacha, Filmmaker

What do you do?

I'm an award-winning filmmaker who is also passionate about teaching and learning new things.

How did you get started in video?

I've always loved photography, films, and radio. I started as a photojournalist at newspapers, then magazines, working my way up to *LIFE* and *National Geographic*. About 10 years ago, the world of magazines started to shrink and video for the Web was a wide-open empty space that no one wanted to visit when I started. So I jumped in.

What kinds of stories work best for video?

My mantra for video stories is to find stories that have motion and emotion. I'm not a fan of the talking head video. I'd rather spend my time on Facebook than watch someone talking on screen.

What three tips would you give videographers in terms of finding and reporting video-worthy stories?

Find a strong compelling character that people can relate to, film them doing something other than talking (I like to think of it as filming an "unfolding

Figure 2.10
Bob Sacha, filmmaker.

action"), and look for a conflict or complication or unanswered question that you will resolve. Simplify or answer your question by the end of your video.

How do you get someone to open up to you on camera? How do you get them to forget that the camera is there?
To get the subject to forget you and the gear, you need to be focused on the subject. This means using your gear needs to be intuitive. Don't interview someone but rather have a conversation with your subject. If they give you a bad answer, it's because you asked a bad question. So think about asking smart questions.

What are your best three interviewing tricks?
Listen, listen, listen. Follow your gut: if you're interested, it's likely the audience will be interested, too. Stack your questions in twos and threes. Listen like an editor: if the answer isn't complete, circle back and ask the question again.

When you are in the field, what is in your gear bags?
I shot with a Canon 5D for a long time but now I'm working with a Canon C100. I used Canon gear because I have the lenses and I find the cameras are ergonomic and intuitive. For lenses, I concentrate on IS lenses because they're stabilized and smoother when I'm on a monopod or hand held. My main lens is a 24–105mm f/4 IS lens. Then I have a 70–200mm f/4 IS lens, a 100mm macro IS, and a 35mm f/2 IS for low light situations. I also carry a

Lectrosonics wireless microphone transmitter and receiver with a Tram micro-phone and a vampire clip. I have a Sennheiser shotgun microphone on top of the camera all the time. I also carry spare batteries and extra cards, a Clif Bar, plus a pen and a small notebook.

How do you organize your material in post-production?
I sync interviews and transcribe all of them with the time code every minute. I organize footage by keywords and in bins. I also have a wow bin for the best shots. Staying organized is super critical for editing. I name all my sequences and bins.

You produce for a lot of different organizations. In general, what works best for Web video?
I'm always looking for compelling, emotional stories with a universal connection.

What overall advice would you give to new video producers?
Make lots of work. It's the best way to get better.

Production and Post-Production Techniques

CHAPTER 3

Understanding Exposure, Composition, and Sequences

Video cameras come in all shapes, sizes, and prices. They all boast different options and feature sets. It would be impossible to cover the entire range of cameras on the market in this textbook. Rather, we will focus on understanding the core fundamentals of using *any* video camera to produce professional footage: sensor sizes, video file formats, lenses, exposure, composition, color management, audio, and process or sequence shooting. As a video producer, you must thoroughly understand these concepts to capture usable footage. With practice, you will be able to use these concepts to produce creative, compelling, and beautiful video.

Figure 3.1

Video cameras come in all shapes, sizes, feature sets, and prices.

Figure 3.2
A comparison of various sensor sizes.
Illustration: *Juanita Ceballos*

CAMERA SENSOR SIZE

Full frame
APS-H
APS-C
APS-C
1.5"
MFT 4/3"
1"
1/1.2"
2/3"
1/1.7"
1/2.3"
1/3.2"

24mm

Sensors. Video cameras are often referred to by the size of their sensor (full-frame, APS-C, Super 35mm, 2/3", 1/3", and so on). The sensor is an element of the camera that captures the light or image coming through the lens. The sensor converts light into digital information that the camera stores on memory cards or hard drives. The size and quality of the camera's sensor affects the quality of the image recorded. Typically, large sensors can capture more light, improving the camera's low light performance. The sensor's size can also affect other properties of the image, such as depth-of-field.

Video file formats. Like film stock and analog tape formats, digital video file formats, called *codecs*, can change from camera to camera. H.264, H.265, and AVCHD are some commonly used codecs today. Codecs record video at varying quality and file sizes, and not all codecs will work with all editing systems. It is important to understand which codec your camera uses to avoid compatibility problems in post-production. Certain codecs provide better color depth and image reproduction than others, important factors when deciding which cameras to use for your projects. Codecs are modified and improved regularly. It is important to read the technical specifications of your cameras before you use them. Some broadcast outlets will not accept video that was not shot on an approved codec.

Figure 3.3
Understanding various video codecs is important for capturing and editing footage.
Illustration: *Juanita Ceballos*

UNDERSTANDING EXPOSURE

Cameras, at their most basic level, record light as an image. A sequence of images creates the appearance of motion in the video file. The level at which light is transmitted and captured onto a sensor is referred to as *exposure*. Properly exposed shots produce clear and detailed footage. Under-exposing shots results in dark or completely black images. Over-exposing shots creates blown out images that lack information or detail. Videographers must learn to properly expose their images or risk recording unusable video.

Stops of light. Exposure is often measured in *stops*, a unit of relative brightness. Adding a stop of light doubles the brightness of the image. Reducing the exposure of your shot by a stop makes the image half as bright. This is an important concept to remember as you learn to properly expose your footage. Lower-end cameras and smartphones typically only offer an automatic exposure mode. In this case, the camera will attempt to properly expose your footage for you. In some situations, auto-exposure will result in unwanted results.

It is best to manually expose your footage to get the proper exposure for all of your shots. If available, use your camera in manual exposure mode. There are some situations when you may want to turn your camera to automatic exposure mode, but in general, videographers use the manual settings of their cameras for greater creative control.

Figure 3.4a

This image is over-exposed. The white areas of the photo are blown out and contain no image data.

Figure 3.4b

This image is under-exposed. The primary subject is too dark to see.

Figure 3.5

The right image is one stop of light brighter than the left image.

Figure 3.6
Using auto-exposure may result in poorly exposed subjects.

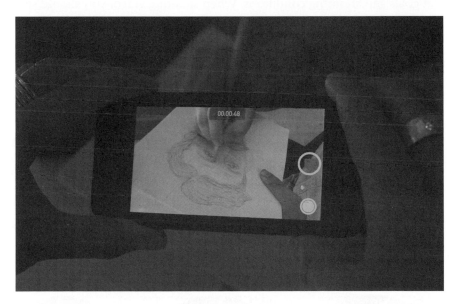

Figure 3.7
The iPhone's default video app does not allow manual exposure.

Shutter speed, ISO, and *aperture* are settings used to adjust exposure on your camera. Lower-end and consumer cameras may not allow you to change these settings. When possible, use a camera that gives you full manual control of shutter speed, ISO, and aperture. There are apps on smartphones that allow for some manual exposure control.

Shutter speed. The shutter is an element of the camera that sits between the lens and the sensor. Shutter speed refers to how fast the shutter of the camera opens and closes while letting light pass through to the sensor. The shutter stays in the closed position until it is triggered to open. When the shutter opens, light passes through and hits the sensor. This light is then recorded as still images or video footage. The shutter then closes again to stop the flow of light. This motion is very much like the blinking of a human eye.

Shutter speed is measured in fractions of a second: 1/60, 1/125, 1/500, 1/1000, and so on. A smaller fraction (for example, 1/1000 of a second) means that the shutter opens and closes more quickly. This lets in less light and results in a darker image. The greater the fraction (for example, 1/60 of a second) means that the shutter stays open for a longer amount of time. This produces a brighter image. When the speed of the shutter is decreased from, for example, 1/1000 to 1/500, the image has *gained one stop of light*. The image is now twice as bright as it was before. This is because the shutter remains open twice as long at 1/500 of a second than it does at 1/1000 of a second.

Still photographers change their shutter speed depending on various editorial goals and shooting conditions. When shooting video, you should set your shutter speed at this ratio: 1/(2 × the frame rate). For example, if you are shooting at 24 frames per second (fps), your shutter speed should be set to 1/48. This number is based on the *180 Degree Shutter Rule*, a convention dating back to the old days of film projectors. This ratio creates footage that most

Figure 3.8

The lens's aperture blades control the amount of light that passes through to the sensor. Shutter speed dictates how long the shutter is open for the light to travel to the sensor.

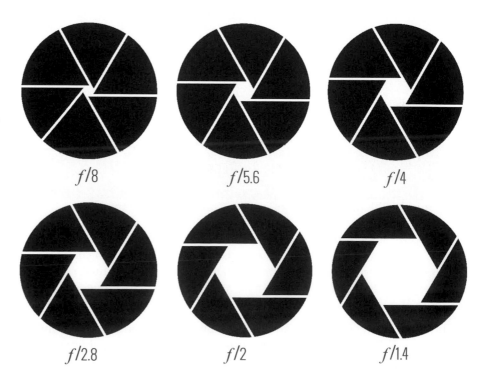

1/500   1/1000

Figure 3.9
The image on the right was shot at a shutter speed of 1/1000, twice as fast as the image on the left shot at a shutter speed of 1/500.

Figure 3.10
A shutter speed that is too low can create unwanted ghosting in your footage.

closely mimics the motion blurring seen in cinema. A faster shutter speed will result in footage that appears to stutter. A slower shutter speed will result in blurry or ghosting images. Occasionally, videographers will use different shutter speeds to get specific visual effects. But, in general, this should be avoided.

ISO. The ISO metric was named after the International Standards Organization, the group that developed the standard for measuring the speed, or light sensitivity, of film. While we shoot digital video these days, we still use the term *film speed*, or ISO, to discuss sensitivity to light. *Note: some cameras use the term "gain" in place of ISO.* If you have ever used a film camera, you will remember loading it with film rated at 200, 400, or 800 ISO. This was the film's speed. Higher film speed means that the film is more sensitive to light and can produce usable images even in lower light conditions.

In the digital world, we still use ISO settings as a way to change the brightness of the image. Instead of using physical film, the camera's sensor and software determines the ISO setting. Manufacturers are constantly improving ISO performance in their cameras. These days, high-end video cameras can go up to nearly 500,000 ISO and still provide a clean image.

How does ISO affect the brightness and quality of your image? Like in the days of film, as you increase the ISO, you increase the brightness of the image. One major trade off is that images tend to get grainier or lower quality as you increase the ISO. In situations that require shooting in a dimly lit environment, you may need to increase your ISO substantially. As you increase the ISO on the camera, you will be able to see the image get brighter. But if you push the ISO setting too high, your image may become too grainy. Higher-end cameras tend to have better ISO performance. This means that, even at high ISO settings, the sensor can preserve the quality of the image.

ISOs work in the same proportion as shutter speeds in terms of stops of light. Remember, a *stop is a measure of relative brightness.* Adding a stop of light will double the brightness of your image. Decreasing exposure by a stop will make the image half as bright. If you double the ISO, you will increase the exposure of

Figure 3.11

Increasing your ISO will produce a brighter image.

the image by one stop, therefore doubling the brightness of your footage. For example, an image shot at 200 ISO will be twice as bright as an image shot at 100 ISO. If that image is shot at 400 ISO, then it will be twice as bright as the image shot at 200 ISO and four times as bright as the image shot at 100 ISO.

The third way to manipulate exposure is in the lens. The *aperture* of the lens is the opening through which light travels to reach the sensor. The aperture of the lens is like the iris of the human eye. As the aperture increases in size, more light travels through to the sensor. This results in a brighter image. As the aperture closes, less light reaches the sensor. In this case, a darker image is produced.

In photography and videography, aperture is measured by its f-number or *f-stop*. Common f-stops are: f/1.4, f/2, f/2.8, f/4, f/5.6, f/8, f/11, f/16, and so on. These numbers, based on a ratio between the lens's focal length and diameter of the aperture opening, can be confusing to new shooters. But you must learn how aperture works to be able to control light. Like shutter speed and ISO, f-stops can be used to calculate and adjust the exposure of your image. For example, f/2.8 is a stop brighter than f/4, meaning that it is twice as bright. F/2.8 is two stops brighter than f/5.6, or four times as bright.

Figure 3.12
Your aperture will affect your exposure, but it will also affect your depth-of-field. Notice that wider apertures result in a blurrier background.

Still photographers manipulate shutter speed, ISO, and aperture to achieve proper exposure. Videographers typically set their shutter speed (using the 180 Degree Shutter Rule) once, but adjust ISO and aperture constantly during shooting. Remember that ISO settings can have effects on your image other than exposure. Higher ISOs will result in grainier footage, and pushing the ISO too high can result in unusable video. Changing the aperture of the lens can change the exposure of the image, but it can also change the *depth-of-field*.

Depth-of-field. Depth-of-field refers to the distance between the closest and farthest objects in an image that appear to be in acceptable focus. In Figure 3.13, you will see that the box is in focus while the camera lens behind it appears soft or out of focus. If I increase the f-stop to f/16, the lens is now in focus. As a rule, increasing the f-stop will result in a greater depth-of-field, or area of acceptable focus. If you shoot at a higher f-stop, more of your image from foreground to background will be in focus. As noted earlier, increasing the f-stop will also make the aperture smaller. Making the aperture smaller decreases the amount of light that passes through to the sensor. This results in a darker image. To compensate for this loss of light, you must increase the ISO to achieve proper exposure.

When you want to decrease the depth-of-field, you must decrease the f-stop (or make the f-number smaller). Decreasing the depth-of-field allows you to

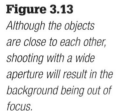

Figure 3.13

Although the objects are close to each other, shooting with a wide aperture will result in the background being out of focus.

Figure 3.14
At a narrow aperture, both the front and background objects are in focus.

highlight a specific element in your shot, while blurring the other objects in front and behind it. This is often called shooting with *shallow* depth-of-field. By decreasing your f-stop, you will also increase the amount of light that can pass through the lens and strike the sensor. This will result in a brighter image. In some cases, a wider aperture will result in over-exposed footage. To reduce the brightness of light in the image, you must reduce the ISO to achieve proper exposure. The important thing to remember is that if you increase light by one stop with your ISO setting, you must decrease it by one stop of light with your aperture. The reverse is also true. This is a common interplay between ISO and aperture that videographers must manage while they shoot.

Neutral density (ND) filter. Occasionally, reducing your ISO and closing your aperture still results in an image that is too bright or over-exposed. This may happen if you shoot in bright or sunny locations. In these cases, you must use a *neutral density*, or *ND*, filter to reduce the amount of light hitting the sensor. Neutral density filters act much like sunglasses for your camera, but they have theoretically have no effect on the quality and color of your footage. Some cameras have built-in ND filters of varying strength. If your camera does not have ND filters, I recommend that you purchase ND filters to be placed over your lenses.

Zebra lines. Some cameras feature *zebra lines* to help shooters determine proper exposure. These lines will appear on areas of your footage that are becoming

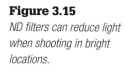

Figure 3.15

ND filters can reduce light when shooting in bright locations.

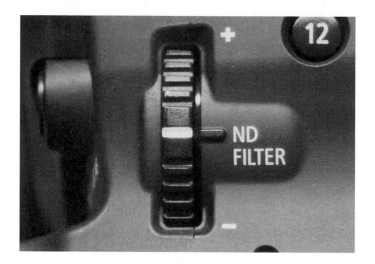

over-exposed. Although you should aim to properly expose all of your footage, it is more important to avoid over-exposing your shots than under-exposing them. Over-exposed footage contains no data and cannot be recovered in post-production. Slightly under-exposed footage is salvageable with some color correction.

Exercise
1. Set your camera to shoot at 24, 25, or 30 frames per second (depending on your preference).
2. Set your shutter speed to the appropriate setting (1/48 for 24fps, 1/50 for 25fps, and 1/60 for 30fps).
3. Set your camera on a tripod and shoot a scene with your ISO set at 800.
4. Adjust your aperture until you get a properly exposed image. What f-stop are you using?
5. Now, set your ISO to 1600. Adjust your aperture until you get a properly exposed image. What f-stop are you using?
6. Finally, set your ISO at 3200. Adjust your aperture until you get a properly exposed image. What f-stop are you using?

Did the f-stop increase or decrease and by how many stops in each set?

High contrast situations. There will be situations where not all areas of the footage will be properly exposed. For example, you may have a person in an interview with a window in the shot. In this case, it is important to expose for the person or main subject of your shot. This may cause you to over-expose the window. If you expose for the window in the shot, your source will be too dark. You must always be sure to properly expose for the main subject of your shot.

It is difficult to shoot in areas with high contrasting lights and darks. For example, if you are shooting outdoors, the areas in the shade will be significantly darker than the areas not shaded by a tree. Exposing for the area that is shaded will cause the other areas of your shot to be over-exposed. Conversely, exposing for the uncovered area of your shot will make the area under the tree very dark.

Figure 3.16a
The subject is properly exposed, but the background is blown out.

Figure 3.16b
The background is properly exposed, but the subject is under-exposed.

Tip: When you need to shoot outdoors (if your production schedule permits), shoot right after dawn or right before sunset. At these times, the sun is lower in the sky and the light is softer and more diffused. Additionally, the colors of the sky are brilliant at these hours. Overcast or cloudy days are also good opportunities for shooting outside. Clouds act like a diffuser for the sun's harsh lights. Your scene will be evenly lit and easier to expose.

Figure 3.17

Shooting at dawn or at the end of the day will result in soft golden colors in your footage.

Exercise

Repeat this exercise in 10 different locations, both indoors and out. Place an object in the middle of your shot. For example, you can use a flower vase or a book. Move your subject from location to location and adjust your ISO and aperture so that your subject is properly exposed. Start with the proper shutter speed for your frame rate, pick a beginning ISO (800 is a good start), and then adjust your aperture to achieve proper exposure. Which situations gave you the most evenly exposed footage?

White balance. White balancing a camera ensures that you are capturing footage with the proper colors. Cameras determine proper color reproduction based on the light source illuminating your shot. Light sources can be natural such as the sun, or artificial such as fluorescent or incandescent lights.

Some cameras have presets for daylight balance (often denoted with a sun icon) or tungsten balance (a lamp). Some allow you to select the specific color temperature, measured in degrees Kelvin (K), of your light source. Improperly white balancing a camera will result in footage that is too blue or too orange in cast. For example, when you are shooting outside, you must shoot with the sun setting, or about 5600 K. When you are shooting indoors using house lights, you must use the tungsten setting, or about 3200 K. You must reset your balance whenever you change locations or shoot under a different light source. Refer to your camera's manual for instructions on how to adjust white balance.

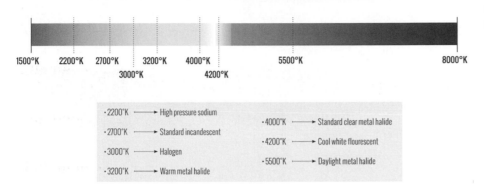

Figure 3.18
Different light sources have different Kelvin temperatures.

COMPOSITION

With the advent of inexpensive video cameras and smartphones, nearly everyone has some experience shooting video these days. However, most people do not know how to shoot professional-quality video. Professional-quality footage means that the video has been properly exposed and composed. *Composing* an image requires the thoughtful and active application of compositional rules when framing a shot. Haphazardly shot or un-composed footage looks amateurish and can often be confusing to the viewer.

From a very early age, we are taught how to read and write. We are taught grammar and the elements of sentence construction: nouns, verbs, adverbs, subjects, objects, and so on. Sentences, paragraphs, essays, and books are compositions of words and punctuation to create greater meaning. Similarly, images and shots need to be carefully composed to give your footage more value.

Unfortunately, very little instruction about visual composition is provided in our school systems. It can be difficult to articulate in words what makes a good shot. Good-looking images are built on solid compositional techniques, just as good writing is based on strong grammar and style. Composition rules range from the very basic to highly sophisticated. We will focus on the basic fundamentals of composition. As you become a more experienced shooter, you will be able to experiment with your own visual style and voice.

The goal of composing any image is to make sense of the objects or information in your frame. Composing images takes *active* decision-making. Most untrained shooters simply point and shoot. As a professional videographer,

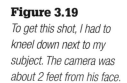

Figure 3.19

To get this shot, I had to kneel down next to my subject. The camera was about 2 feet from his face.

you must work to help the viewer understand the images they are watching. This may require you to spend a considerable amount of time contemplating your shots before you hit record. You may need to walk around, kneel down, climb on a ladder, and shoot from a position that is not naturally comfortable.

Camera placement. The first step in creating a visual composition is deciding on camera placement. Where you put your camera, where it is pointed, and how high or low it sits all affect your composition. Most amateur videographers shoot almost exclusively at eye-level. Videographers jokingly call this 5′7″ disease. To achieve a variety of shots, you must think creatively.

- *Get low.* Shooting from any height other than eye-level will present an interesting perspective for the viewer. Most people do not crouch down or bring their eyes to table- or floor-level. These shots can produce interesting results.
- *Shoot from the hip.* There is the popular image on TV and in the movies of camera operators holding cameras on their shoulders. While this is a common shooting posture, there is no rule that says you have to shoot only in this position. Move your camera to hip-level or directly in front of your chest for a different perspective. Shooting your subject from below will make your subject seem larger. Holding your camera lower can be more comfortable and stable.

Figure 3.20a
A videographer shooting low for an interesting angle.

Figure 3.20b
A videographer shooting from the hip rather than from eye-level.

- *Get high.* Shooting from above can also give your footage a unique perspective. Shoot on apple boxes, chairs, and ladders. If it is safe, shoot from windows and rooftops. Footage shot from up high can give your viewer a better sense of the size of a location. Shooting a person or object from up high can make your subject seem smaller.
- *Point-of-view (POV).* Point-of-view shots represent the vantage point of a particular character in your story. For example, if you are shooting a discussion between two characters, you might want to shoot the first character at eye-level, positioning yourself directly behind the second character. This creates the effect of watching the scene from the second character's point-of-view.

Figure 3.20c

A videographer shooting from a high angle for an interesting shot.

Figure 3.20d

A videographer shoots over the subject's shoulder to mimic the subject's point-of-view.

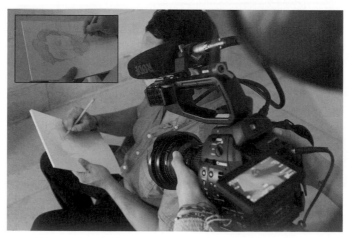

Exercise
Choose a person or any object and shoot your subject from eye-level. Next, shoot the same subject from hip-level. Then shoot from down low. Finally, shoot your subject from at least 5 feet above eye-level. How does the look of your subject change from each perspective? How can you create different moods with each angle? Does the subject seem to change in size depending on your camera placement?

Creating order. A photographer friend once told me that *composition* is simply making visual sense of the chaos around us. Careful composition creates order in your footage. To compose an image well, you must force yourself to think about the goals of each shot. What do you want your viewer to focus on? What is of importance? Actively composing your image requires you to decide what to highlight in your shot and what to diminish.

Once you have decided on the camera's vantage point, you must then choose which elements or objects to keep in the frame and which to leave out. There are many compositional rules you can use to help you achieve better shots. These techniques may force you to frame your shot in different ways—by moving the camera forward or backwards, *panning* left or right, or *tilting* up and down.

There are many compositional techniques, but we will focus on the most basic and effective ones for non-fiction videography:

- Rule of Thirds
- Environmental Framing
- Lines
- Selective Focus (Shallow Depth-of-Field)
- Close Ups

Rule of Thirds. Inexperienced photographers and videographers have a tendency of centering their images. This technique creates dull or flat results in your footage. The *Rule of Thirds*, a classic compositional technique used in photography, graphic arts, and design, can be used to increase tension and energy in your images.

The Rule of Thirds is executed by dividing your frame into nine equal segments with two lines running vertically and two lines running horizontally, similar to a tic-tac-toe board. Rather than placing the primary subject of your image squarely in the center of the frame, the subject should be moved to one of the points where the horizontal and vertical lines intersect. Any of these four intersecting points can be used.

Figure 3.21

This image has been shot using the Rule of Thirds.

Figure 3.22

These grid lines show that the source falls on the upper-right third of the image.

Figure 3.23a

The subject is in the upper-left third of the frame.

Figure 3.23b
The subject is in the upper-right third of the frame.

Figure 3.23c
The subject is in the lower-left third of the frame.

Figure 3.23d
The subject is in the lower-right third of the frame.

The Rule of Thirds is one of the most basic compositional techniques used in photography and video. However, it requires the shooter to actively frame the shot in a specific way that enhances the image. Note that your subject can be large or small in the frame, as long as your subject remains at one of the intersecting points.

Figure 3.24a
The Rule of Thirds can be applied to wide shots.

Figure 3.24b
The Rule of Thirds can be applied to close up shots.

Exercise

Go to 10 different locations. Select a primary subject that you want to shoot. This can be a person or any object. Frame your shot with your subject at one of the four intersection points. Does this result in a more dynamic image?

Environmental framing. Environmental framing is a compositional technique that involves using environmental elements such as doorways, mirrors, plants, people, light, and shapes to highlight the primary subject of your shot. We use picture frames to highlight our favorite photos or works of art. We use spotlights to draw attention to the lead singers during a performance. We can apply these same principals when we compose our footage.

Using environmental shapes to isolate your images is an effective way to make your footage more compelling. Structures such as doorways, fences, tunnels, and windows are stationary and readily available in most situations. As a videographer, you have to actively look for these opportunities. This may require walking around and analyzing your environment at length before you start shooting. An untrained shooter points and shoots where it is convenient; a professional videographer takes time to compose. Placing your subjects within an architectural frame draws the viewer's eye to the subject. This helps to create a shot that is less visually complicated and much easier for the viewer to understand.

Figure 3.25
The subject is framed by the mirror, an element of the environment.

Exercise

Go to 10 different locations and find opportunities for environmental frames. These can be mirrors, windows, openings in walls or fences, the curved handle of a coffee cup, or anywhere where an object creates a frame. Most locations will provide several architectural frames. Position your camera so that the opening in the frame completely surrounds the subject of your shot. Record a few seconds of each shot. How long did it take you to find these frames? Did you have to place your camera higher or lower than you normally would?

Lines. Video works in two dimensions. That is to say: the frame of your shot has a width and a height. One goal of the videographer is to create depth, or the illusion of a third dimension in your footage. Lines and patterns naturally existing in the environment can be used to create depth. They can also be used to draw the viewer's eye to your primary subject.

Shooting a building straight on (at a 90 degree angle) will result in a very flat image. Instead, position your camera at a smaller angle in relation to the building to create an image with greater perceived depth. By shooting flat objects on an angle, you can create lines that appear to head towards a vanishing point. Shooting a street from the side does not connote depth, but shooting it from a low angle down will create a greater sense and appearance of three dimensions.

Figure 3.26a

This shot of a building is flat and dull.

Figure 3.26b
This shot of a building shows depth and gives the viewer more environmental information.

Figure 3.27
Shooting a street from a low angle will create dramatic depth in your images.

Lines help draw the viewer's eye towards the primary subject of your shot, and they can lead your viewer to look at a particular portion of the image. This technique, like the Rule of Thirds and architectural framing, can be used to highlight your subject and eliminate visual confusion or noise for the viewer.

Exercise

Go to 10 different locations and find opportunities for shooting lines. These can be fences, rows of buildings, computer monitors, parking meters, and so on. There are lines everywhere in any environment. Position your camera and compose your shot to produce an image with depth. Record a few seconds of each shot. How long did it take you to find these lines and execute these shots? Did you have to reposition your camera many times to achieve greater depth?

Selective focus (shallow depth-of-field). Earlier, we discussed the concept of depth-of-field. Depth-of-field is the distance between the closest and farthest objects in an image that appear to be in acceptable focus. Controlling depth-of-field can help you to isolate the primary subject of your shot by blurring out elements of less importance. Increasing your f-stop makes your aperture smaller and results in a great depth-of-field. Conversely, decreasing your f-stop will result in a wider aperture and a shallower depth-of-field.

New shooters can initially have a hard time understanding how to control depth-of-field. If you do get confused, think about the human eye. If you cannot see something far away, you will tend to squint, effectively reducing the aperture of your eyes. This increases your eyes' depth-of-field. When you do this, you can see at a further distance. Your lens works in the same way: smaller apertures result in a longer depth-of-field. Wider apertures (smaller f-stop) reduce the depth-of-field.

Note: As mentioned earlier, when you adjust your aperture, you may need to adjust your ISO as well to maintain proper exposure.

Look at Figures 3.28a, 3.28b, and 3.28c. You will see that, although the two people in the shot stay in the same position, changing the aperture will allow

Figure 3.28a

The aperture and focus have been set to isolate the subject in the foreground.

Figure 3.28b
The aperture and focus have been set to isolate the subject in the background.

Figure 3.28c
The aperture and the focus have been set to show both the foreground and background subjects.

you to focus on the person in the front, the person in the back, or both. Along with aperture, sensor size affects your depth-of-field. Bigger sensors produce footage with shallower depth-of-field.

Shallow depth-of-field can work great for shooting objects that stay still, such as buildings, plants, and street signs. However, if you are shooting moving objects, it is best that you do not make your shots too shallow and risk losing focus. When shooting on an APS-C, Super 35mm, or larger sensor camera, do not shoot wider than f/5.6. Shooting at f/4 or f/2.8 or wider will produce footage that goes in and out of focus too much. When you are starting to learn how to shoot video, it is best to shoot with greater depth-of-field. Start shooting at f/8 or higher.

There are many free or inexpensive online and mobile depth-of-field calculators available. These tools will help you to calculate how much focusing area you have at certain apertures using different cameras. For example, when shooting on a full-frame sensor camera at an aperture of f/5.6 with a 50mm lens with my subject 10 feet away from me, I only have a depth-of-field of 4.28 feet. If I change my f-stop to f/11, my depth-of-field increases to 9.6 feet, meaning that a larger portion of my image will likely stay in focus. Using depth-of-field calculators is a great way to begin to understand the relationship between aperture and its effect on depth-of-field. But the best

Figure 3.29

There are many depth-of-field calculators available for your computer or smartphone.

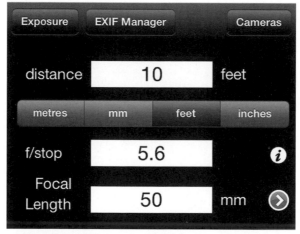

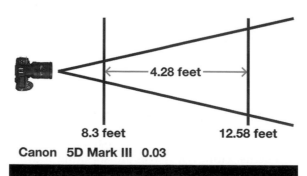

way to understand any of these camera concepts is to go out and shoot as much as possible.

Exercise

Line up five objects on a table, placing each object about 1 foot behind the previous object. Position your camera about 2 feet in front of the first object on the table. Focus on the front object and adjust your aperture so that the other objects are out of focus. Then adjust your ISO so that your shot is properly exposed.

Adjust your aperture until only the first and second objects are in focus. Did the image get darker? Did you have to adjust your ISO? Adjust your aperture until the first, second, and third objects are in focus, but the other objects are not. What are your aperture and ISO settings? Repeat this exercise until all objects are in focus. What are your aperture and ISO settings? You should see a relation between increasing depth-of-field and increasing ISO.

CLOSE UPS

The term *close up* is a relative one. One videographer's close up may appear to be a medium shot to another shooter. But, in general, in a close up, the primary subject of your shot fills more than half of your entire frame. Close ups provide great detail: the wrinkles on someone's hand, the detail of flowers, the texture of sand. By filling the frame with your primary subject, you are eliminating all other confusing or unnecessary elements. Close ups are a simple but very effective compositional technique that produces great footage.

Getting close enough for a close up can be surprisingly difficult for a new shooter. Moving close to someone with a camera takes discipline. When we shoot family vacation photos or iPhone videos, we tend to stand at least 8 feet or more away from our subjects. Getting any closer can feel like an invasion of personal space. A videographer will often have to get within inches of his subject. While you can zoom on your camera to get closer, this is not always a preferred technique. We will discuss how to shoot close ups in more detail in Chapter 5: Field Production.

Exercise

Go to 10 different locations and shoot close ups of your primary subject. In this exercise, try to shoot people. When you are starting out as a shooter, it is very uncomfortable to get close to people. You must practice often to overcome this fear and hesitation. During this exercise, do not use the zoom on your camera. Move closer to your subject with your feet.

UNDERSTAND FOCAL LENGTHS

The *focal length* of a lens is the distance between the lens and the camera's sensor when the image is focused to infinity. Focal length is measured in millimeters, such as 24mm, 35mm, 85mm, and so on. Lenses with a fixed focal length are called *prime* lenses. *Zoom* lenses have adjustable focal lengths. Zoom lenses feature minimum and maximum focal lengths such as 24–70mm, 24–105mm, 70–200mm, and so on.

The focal length of the lens affects the *field of view* (also known as the angle of view), or what is visible in the frame of your shot. A shorter focal length results in a wider field of view, whereas a longer focal length results in a narrower field of view. When you zoom in on your subject, you are decreasing your field of view and limiting the elements in your frame. This creates the illusion that you are physically closer to your image.

Using different focal lengths can dramatically affect your image in ways other than simply magnifying your subject. *Wide-angle* lenses (such as 24mm or shorter) give your shots a wide field of view, but they also exaggerate the foreground of your shot. *Normal* lenses (such as a 50mm lens) present an angle of view that looks natural or "normal" to the human eye. Telephoto lenses (85mm and longer) give a narrower angle of view and compress the foreground and background in your shot.

Figures 3.32a, 3.32b, and 3.32c are images of the same scene, but each was shot with a different lens: a wide-angle lens (24mm), a normal lens

Figure 3.30
Illustration: *Juanita Ceballos*

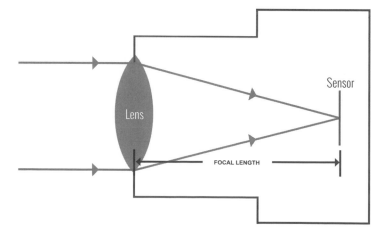

FOCAL LENGTH

Figure 3.31a
A shorter focal length (24mm) creates a wider field-of-view.

Figure 3.31b
A longer focal length (105mm) creates a narrower field-of view.

(50mm), and a telephoto lens (105mm). In each shot, the foreground object has been framed to be in the same position and size. Notice what happens to the appearance of the background object. In the 24mm shot, the background object seems to be at a great distance away from the

Figure 3.32a
This image was shot at a focal length of 24mm.

Figure 3.32b
This image was shot at a focal length of 50mm.

foreground object. In the 105mm shot, the background object seems much closer to the foreground object. In the 50mm shot, the foreground and background objects seem to be the same relative size as they would appear to the human eye.

Understanding focal lengths and their effects on your image will allow you to make creative and editorial decisions in your compositions. For example, if you use a wide-angle lens to shoot a scene of two people

Exposure, Composition, and Sequences

Figure 3.32c
This image was shot at a focal length of 105mm.

Figure 3.33a
In this image (shot at 24mm), the person on the left seems significantly smaller than the person on the right.

having a conversation, then the person in the background will appear to be much smaller than the person in the foreground. This may make the foreground subject seem much more impressive or powerful. If you shoot the same scene with a normal or telephoto lens, the two people will appear to be more proportionally balanced. Wide-angle lenses can also make shots very dramatic, and ultra-wide angle lenses can make your images appear skewed.

Figure 3.33b

In this image (shot at 85mm), the two people seem to be proportional in size.

Figure 3.34

Shooting with shorter focal lengths can produce dramatic wide-angle shots.

Practice shooting with different focal lengths to understand the effects they can have on your shots. While focal length is primarily used to zoom in or zoom out of a scene, it is important to understand that different lenses can have dramatic editorial impact on your footage.

Exercise

1. Select a scene to shoot. Decide on a foreground object. This can be a person, a sign, or any other object. Frame and focus on this object using a wide-angle lens. Shoot a few seconds of this shot.
2. Adjust your lens to a normal length (such as 50mm). You will notice that your field of view has changed and your foreground object appears closer in your shot. Adjust the position of your camera so that your foreground object is in the same position and same size as it was in your wide-angle shot. How far back did you have to move your camera? Shoot a few seconds of this shot.
3. Adjust your lens to a telephoto length (such as 100mm). You will notice that your field of view has changed again and your foreground object appears much closer in your shot. Adjust the position of your camera so that the foreground object is in the same place and is the same size as it was in your wide- and normal-angle shots. How far back did you have to move your camera? Shoot a few seconds of this shot.
4. Review your footage. How did the background objects of your shot change when you adjusted your focal length?

THINGS TO AVOID

There are some mistakes that all new videographers repeatedly make in the field. Most of these errors require practice and experience to avoid. The key to becoming a great videographer is to shoot as much as possible—you must pick up your camera and shoot stories or practice every day. When you are shooting, pay special attention to these common mistakes and double check that you are not making these errors.

Forgetting to hit record. Before shooting a single frame of footage, videographers must be concerned with sensors, codecs, shutter speed, ISO, aperture, and composition. This can be overwhelming and can cause you to forget to hit record. Yes, this happens all the time. Even experienced shooters make this mistake. I have been guilty of this on *many* occasions. The only way to avoid

Figure 3.35

Be sure to check that your record light is on when recording.

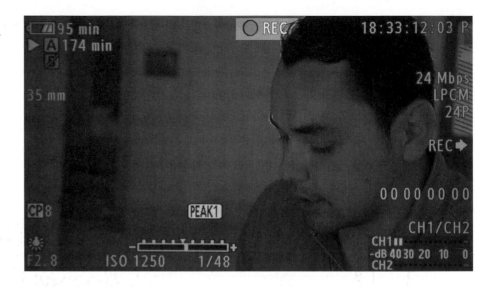

Figure 3.36

Back-lit scenes can result in under-exposed subjects.

this is by being diligent about checking that the record light is on and that the time code on the camera is spinning forward.

Back lighting. Back lighting, as the terms implies, means having a light source behind the primary subject of your shot. This can happen, for example, when an interview subject is placed in front of a bright window. Back lighting will cause exposure problems. You will under-expose your subject or you will over-expose the light source. Neither result is ideal.

Missing focus. Out-of-focused footage is unusable footage. Keeping the subject of your shot in focus requires great concentration. Many cameras have focusing tools to assist in achieving sharp images. *Peaking* is a feature that highlights your image with a color outline of the areas where your shot is in focus. Some cameras allow you to digitally zoom in your shot to see if the image is sharp or soft. Learn to use the focusing tools on your camera to ensure proper focus.

Incorrectly white balancing. Shooters often forget to set the white balance on their cameras before recording. The wrong white balance setting will result in footage with a strong blue or orange cast. While colors can be adjusted in most editing software, you should aim to get proper colors in your original footage. Be sure to white balance your camera every time your light source changes. If you go from an office to a hallway, you may need to reset your white balance. If you go from inside a home to the backyard, you will need to reset your white balance. Learn how to adjust white balance quickly on your camera so that you will not miss shooting opportunities. Even if you are in a rush, set aside time to properly white balance your footage. This will save you much time and frustration later.

Poor posture and support. Videography is a challenging physical activity. To reduce fatigue or risk of injury, you must hold your camera properly. If your camera is too heavy for you, use additional supports such as monopods or tripods. These supports will not only reduce strain on your back and shoulders, but they will also provide steadier shots.

Figure 3.37
Some cameras feature peaking functions (the red lines on the subject) that aid in achieving focus.

Figure 3.38a

The videographer is holding the camera too far away from her body. This will quickly cause her arms to fatigue.

Figure 3.38b

The videographer is holding the camera close to her body. This will allow her to use her body.

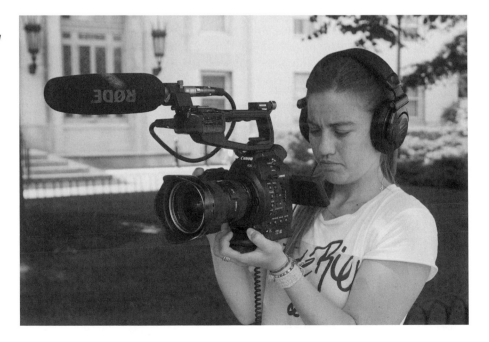

Figure 3.39
Use tripods and monopods to achieve steady footage, especially on long shoots.

SHOOTING PROCESS

Video is a sequence of still images that, when played quickly, creates motion. Video is its most effective when your story features action—athletes playing sports, construction workers building houses, doctors treating patients, and so on. Video is ineffective when your imagery is motionless or does not possess enough visual variety. Interview-heavy or *talking head* videos are boring for viewers and do not maximize the power of the medium. To tell successful visual stories, you must be able to identify opportunities for shooting motion. Once you have determined which processes to shoot, you must learn to shoot in a way that will yield enough material for editing compelling sequences later.

Inexperienced videographers often make the mistake of shooting too much footage or shooting without planning or clear goals. To gather enough high-quality, meaningful footage for your video stories, you must:

- *Identify the real action you want to capture.* For example, a football player may talk about the challenges of being a professional athlete. You will naturally want to shoot the football game, but you must also capture the player lifting weights, working out with his trainer, working with the media, and dealing with fans. You must determine *all* the action that pertains to your story, not just the obvious scenes.
- *Determine the best time and location to shoot.* In a profile of a master sushi chef, it is may be best to shoot a cooking demonstration when the restaurant is closed to avoid crowd noise and other distractions (for you and for the chef). It may make more sense to shoot the demonstration at his home where there is more room than in his small restaurant kitchen. When possible, do a location scout of potential venues before your shoot.
- *Acquire all necessary rights and permissions to shoot at your location.* A teacher may give you access to shoot in her classroom, but she may not have the proper authority to grant you permission. You may be required to get permission from the principal, the Board of Education, or the parents of the students. Be sure you have secured all rights and permissions to shoot, or you may be denied access when you arrive at the location.
- *Make sure you have enough time to shoot.* Shooting, as a rule, always takes longer than you think. Composition takes time. Proper lighting takes time. Getting enough footage takes time. Each story and location will be different, but always schedule enough time for yourself and your source to get enough material. As you become a more experienced shooter, you will become better at gauging how much time you need for each shoot.
- *Make sure you have properly working equipment.* Be sure to have properly functioning equipment with you. Check your batteries and your camera before you leave for your shoot. Check that your tripods and microphones are working. Turn on all your equipment and record a test clip before you head out into the field.
- *Shoot complete sequences.* Once you have learned how to compose individual shots, you must learn how to shoot footage in a series that makes sense. Shooting complete sequences or processes is key to acquiring enough footage to tell your story later.

SHOOTING SEQUENCES

Life happens in real time. In video, we only have a limited number of minutes to tell our story. For example, an artist may require 8 hours to finish drawing a picture. You may only have 30 seconds in your final video piece to illustrate his process. You must be able to shoot enough elements to give a sense of the process—the drawing of outlines, the tracing of the image with darker inks, the shading, the thoughtful looks on the face of the artist, the corrections she makes, and so on. Each of these elements may only last a few seconds on screen, but you must shoot them to give the viewer a sense of the entire process.

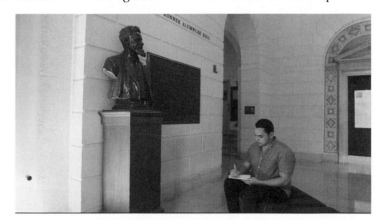

Figure 3.40a
Subject shot from a wide angle.

Figure 3.40b
Subject shot from a medium distance.

Figure 3.40c
Subject shot close up.

Figure 3.40d

Subject shot close up from an alternate angle.

Sequence or process shooting requires planning and discipline. You must get your shots when you are in the field. If you fail to record the action and processes you need, then that footage will not be available for editing in post-production. For example, if the artist uses a special smudging technique in her drawings and you fail to shoot her doing it, then it will be difficult for you to tell that part of the story. This is unlike writing news stories when you can recreate scenes from your notes. A videographer cannot create scenes that he or she did not shoot in the field.

THE 3 × 3 RULE

When I shoot, I follow a simple pattern to ensure that I get footage with enough visual variety. I call it the *3 × 3 Rule*. For every process or action (such as an artist drawing a picture), I identify three angles from which to shoot the subject. At each angle, I shoot the subject from three distances: far away, medium distance, and close up. This will result in three types of shots: wide shots, medium shots, and close ups.

Wide, *medium*, and *close up* are relative terms. A medium shot to one shooter may appear to be a wide shot to another. But, typically, this is how they are defined:

- *Wide shots* (abbreviated as *WS*) put the primary subject of your shot in the larger context of its environment. For example, if you are shooting a professor in a classroom, then a wide shot would show the professor, the students, the desks, and a large portion of the room.
- *Medium shots* (abbreviated as *MS*) put the subject of your shot in context of the environment, but with your subject taking up more visual space in the frame. In the case of the professor, the medium shot may feature the professor and a couple of students. The rest of the class is framed out.

- *Close up shots* (abbreviated as *CU*) fill the frame with your primary subject. In the example of the professor, a close up may be a shot with his face or a shot of a student's hand taking notes. Close ups, as discussed in the section on composition, is an important way to show details in your scenes.

Figure 3.41a
The videographer shoots her subject from a wide angle.

Figure 3.41b
The videographer moves in closer to shoot a medium angle shot.

Figure 3.41c

Rather than zooming, the videographer moves within a couple of feet of the subject to get a close up shot.

Figure 3.41d

The videographer shoots her subject from a different wide angle.

Figure 3.41e

The videographer moves in closer to shoot a medium shot from the new angle.

Figure 3.41f
The videographer moves within a couple of feet of the subject to get a close up shot from the new angle.

The 3 × 3 Rule can be applied for almost any situation. When you have established the first angle, shoot a wide shot. Hold your shot steady for at least 10 seconds. This will ensure that you have enough steady footage from that angle and distance to be used for editing. You can count silently to yourself or watch the time code on the camera's LCD screen. Once you have captured your wide shot, move in to get a medium shot. It is important that you physically move your body and camera closer to the subject, rather than using the camera's zoom function. When shooting handheld or with a monopod, zooming with your camera will result in shaky footage. Once you have held your medium shot for at least 10 seconds, move in closer for your close up shot. This may require you to come as close as within a foot of your subject. This will feel very uncomfortable to you at first. You must force yourself to get close.

Being able to hold your shot for 10 seconds takes practice and discipline. But be sure to hold your shot and resist the temptation to move your camera (even if your subject moves out of frame). Some actions will happen quickly. For example, the professor may ask a question and students will raise their hands quickly to answer. You may want to capture this question-and-answer scene. When you employ the 3 × 3 Rule, you will have to be patient. Your wide shot may be the first question the professor asks. Your medium shot may be the third question. Your close up may be the last question asked. You must look for repeated actions and use them as opportunities to get enough shots to satisfy the 3 × 3 Rule. For example, if you are profiling a chef, your chef will often make the same dish repeatedly. This is a great opportunity to carefully compose your images and still be able to get the various angles you need.

One note about the 3 × 3 Rule: This is just a minimum guideline. If you have the opportunity and time, shoot 4, 5, 6, or more angles. Also, 10 seconds is a minimum length of time to shoot. With each angle, always shoot a wide shot, a medium shot, and a close up. You must discipline yourself to acquire a wide array of shots to able to edit a sequence later.

Exercise

Find a person who is repeating a process. For example, a fruit vendor sells many fruit each day to various customers. Identify the three angles to approach this scene. One angle may be from the right of the vendor. Shoot a wide shot. Hold that shot for 10 seconds. Walk in and shoot a medium shot. Walk in further and shoot a close up of the vendor or some fruit. It is important to get at least 10 seconds of steady footage, whether you are shooting handheld or on a tripod. Pick a second angle. In this case, try shooting from behind the fruit cart. Again, shoot wide, medium, and close up. Then pick a third angle. Review your footage. Which angles and shots worked best?

Panning and tilting. A common mistake that new shooters make is panning or tilting their camera too much. Panning is the act of pivoting your camera left and right. Tilting is pivoting your camera up and down. You will see camera motion such as pans and tilts in amateur videography. As a professional videographer, you should avoid moving the camera during your shot, unless your pans and tilts are *motivated.*

Motivated pans and tilts mean that the motion is executed for an editorial reason. For example, if you pan slowly from one part of the room to the next, you will reveal something unexpected about the second half of the room. Do not use pans to show the different elements of the environment that you are shooting. If you have properly shot footage using the 3 × 3 Rule, you will have many wide, medium, and close ups to give your viewer a clear sense of the environment and your subject.

Tip: I highly recommend that new shooters AVOID panning and tilting. These movements can provide great editorial value to your story, but they are sophisticated and can be hard to execute well by inexperienced shooters. For now, treat each shot as you would a still photo: point at your subject, compose your shot using compositional techniques we have discussed, and hold your shot still as you record action in the shot. Your camera should not move during recording. Rather, the elements in your shot (people, cars, clouds) should be in motion.

Q&A with the Experts: Ben de la Cruz, Multimedia Editor, NPR

Figure 3.42
Ben de la Cruz, Multimedia Editor, NPR.

How did you get started in video?
I produced my first documentary for PBS not too long after I graduated from college. I partnered with a friend who was writing for a PBS show. I didn't know how to shoot or edit, but I like to think that I knew how to tell a story. I didn't learn to shoot and edit until years later when I joined the multimedia team at the *Washington Post* in 2000. It was a job that changed my life. I became part of a groundbreaking team of video journalists, led by our editor Tom Kennedy, who in many ways helped showcase the possibilities of the one-person band model of multimedia reporting. We all learned to edit, shoot, report, write, and produce our own pieces. We all used Final Cut Pro (Version 1!). At this time, our workflow was completely different from the broadcast TV model that counted on a team of specialists—sound engineer, producer, reporter, editor, and photographer—to produce their news and feature reports.

What kinds of stories work best for video?
Video is a terrific medium for capturing emotion, gesture, body language, and action. It's not as good with explaining complex stories as other mediums like a magazine or newspaper story. The videos that excite me are ones that

feature a strong central character doing something filmable directly related to their story—not someone talking about something they've done in the past.

What three tips would you give videographers in terms of finding and reporting video-worthy stories?

Finding stories for video is not all that different than finding good stories for other media. Good stories have strong characters, a narrative arc, and a universal theme that allows readers/viewers to connect to it. But there are some important elements necessary to make a good video.

1. A good video story needs a great character who is comfortable in front of the camera. The character must be open, candid, and a good storyteller in their own right. This will enable the video to have little or no Voice-of-God narration, which will make for a more cinematic experience for the viewer.
2. A good video story features scenes with action/interaction that is directly relevant to the story.
3. A good video story transports the viewer to a place or a state-of-mind that viewers rarely get to see.

How do you get someone to open up to you on camera? How do you get them to "forget" that the camera is there?

Like all reporting, and more so when a person has to be on-camera, getting someone to open up takes time. The short answer is that they have to trust you. You can do that by being knowledgeable about the topic you'll be discussing. This shows that you genuinely care about presenting their story fairly and accurately. The best reporters/interviewers are ones who know how to relate to people. Every time I get this question about how I make people comfortable in front of the camera, I am always reminded of Ben Bradlee, the famed executive editor of the *Washington Post* during Watergate, talking about how reporter Bob Woodward gained the trust of Deep Throat. "He works at it," said Bradlee, "And he's got that broad sort of Midwestern open face. He will look you in the eye. Older people want to adopt him and younger people want to be his pal."

What are your best three interviewing tricks?

Interviewing is about building rapport. A subject must trust you in order for them to give you something personal and candid. The best interviewers are people who can convey to their subject that they genuinely care about the subject. That said, thoroughly preparing for an interview is another key to conducting a good interview. A colleague of mine at NPR, for instance, writes out 100 questions she wants to ask before each interview. The questions are ordered so that they flow into each other, which makes for a natural conversation. I don't think of 100 questions, but I do try to anticipate the flow of conversation. This is not a trick, but more of a general philosophy I try to follow when doing an interview.

When you are in the field, what is in your gear bags?
- Two Canon 5D Mark IIs
- Canon 50mm 1.2 lens
- Canon 70–200mm 2.8 lens
- Canon 16–35mm
- Four 32gb CF cards
- Two 16gb CF cards
- Marantz PMD660—audio recorder
- Zacuto viewfinder
- Rode videomic
- AudioTechnica shotgun mic
- Sony MDR-7506 headphones
- Microphone bracket
- Lots of AAA batteries
- Six Canon 5D batteries and two chargers
- Sennheiser wireless lavalier microphones
- NPR business cards
- Lens spray and cloth
- Two XLR chords
- Two Manfroto lightweight tripods with Manfroto 501HDV and 701HDV tripod heads

How do you organize your material in post-production?
I was never great at organizing files, though working with others on shoots has forced me to come up with a better system. I store files on external hard drives organized by day and by media—audio, video, or stills. I log each interview by using subclips to label them. For foreign language interviews, I send everything out for transcription with time codes.

NPR is starting to define its video tone. What works for NPR in terms of video and what works for Web video in general?
Compared to the *New York Times*, the *Washington Post*, *Vice News*, and other national media outlets, NPR produces very few videos. So when we do produce a video, we make an extra effort to make it special. Our videos try to embody what people in the newsroom refer to as "NPR-ness." Ideally, this means the video is a great story with compelling characters, executed beautifully, and—to paraphrase Jonathan Harris, one of my favorite artists—with a touch of whimsy.

The NPR videos that have been "hits" with our audience vary from fun science videos that blend video and animation to full-blown interactive video apps like Planet Money's T-Shirt Project to NPR's incredibly popular Tiny Desk Concerts.

What overall advice would you give to new video producers?

Practice, practice, practice! Video requires so many skills to master. But don't be discouraged. You'll eventually get there.

CHAPTER 4

Audio

One of the most important rules and greatest ironies of video production is that audio quality is always more important than video quality. While we have spent the last couple of chapters on producing properly exposed and well-composed footage, we must pay even greater attention to producing and recording high-quality audio.

There are three main factors that affect the quality of audio recordings: microphone type, microphone placement, and environmental noise. Videographers must understand how microphones work and how to minimize environmental noise to achieve high-quality audio recordings. In ideal situations, videographers should team up with audio recordists during production. Shooting video—obtaining correct exposure, properly composing shots, and shooting sequences—requires intense concentration. Monitoring and recording audio adds a deeper layer of complexity. Unfortunately, the budgets of many productions these days do not allow for both a videographer and an audio recordist. The videographer is forced to manage both video and audio in the field.

Video journalists typically work with two types of field microphones: dynamic and condenser. These terms refer to how the microphone generates an electronic signal. Using the most basic definitions, dynamic microphones use electromagnetic induction to produce a signal, while condenser microphones require external power from a battery or directly from the camera. Condenser microphones tend to be more responsive than dynamic microphones.

Microphones pick up and ignore audio in different patterns depending on their design. This recording shape is referred to as the microphone's *pick up pattern*. There are several types of pick up patterns: bi-directional, subcardioid, hypercardioid, supercardioid, omnidirectional, cardioid, and shotgun. Understanding these pick up patterns will help you to select the right microphone for your needs. In video production, you will be using mostly microphones with omnidirectional, cardioid, and shotgun pick up patterns.

Shotgun microphones. Shotgun microphones pick up in the shotgun pattern: in front and slightly behind the microphone. They tend to reject the audio

Figure 4.1

Dynamic condenser microphones come in a variety of sizes and pick up patterns.

Figure 4.2

Various microphone pick up patterns.

MICROPHONE PICK UP PATTERN

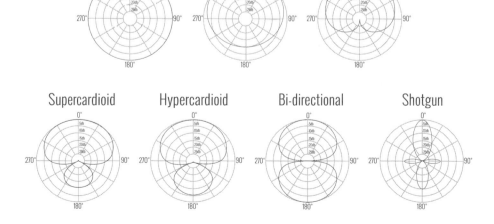

Omnidirectional   Subcardioid   Cardioid

Supercardioid   Hypercardioid   Bi-directional   Shotgun

around the side of the microphone. Shotgun microphones are tubular in shape, but can come in various lengths and widths. They are commonly mounted on the camera, either on the top or on the side. While this is a conventional set up, this is not always the ideal position for the microphone to collect the best audio. When a videographer works with a sound recordist, the shotgun microphone will be placed on a *boom pole*. This allows the sound person to place the shotgun microphone closest to the source of audio, resulting in the cleanest and strongest recording.

Lavalier microphones. Lavalier microphones, often called lav or lapel microphones, are most often used to record voices. They are used in interview settings or during scenes that require clear audio from your source, even in crowded and noisy environments. Lavalier microphones typically have an omnidirectional or cardioid pick up pattern. Lav microphones do not have the same reach as shotgun microphones. They have been designed to be mounted close to the subject's mouth. Omnidirectional microphones can be positioned at various angles, as they will pick up audio from all sides.

Inverse-square law. Microphones pick up sound waves in a proportion known as the *inverse-square law*. Simply put, this means that as microphones are placed closer to the audio source, the sound intensity and recording level will increase exponentially. As they are placed further away from the audio source, the sound intensity will decrease exponentially. For example, if the

Figure 4.3a
Shotgun microphones are typically placed on top of the video camera when a sound recordist is not available.

Figure 4.3b

Lav microphones are used to record high-quality interviews.

Figure 4.4

As a microphone moves away from an audio source, the audio level decreases exponentially.

INVERSE-SQUARE LAW

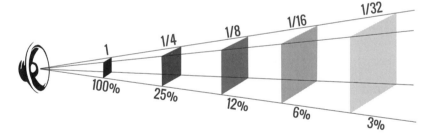

microphone is one foot away from the audio source and is then moved back one foot, the audio intensity will be one-quarter its previous level. If it is moved back another foot, the audio intensity is at one-eighth its original level. As the microphone moves further and further away from the audio source, the audio level diminishes greatly.

To compensate for decreased source audio intensity, you can turn up the recording volume or *gain* on your camera. But note that when you increase the gain on your camera, you are increasing the recording level of all audio sources in the room. You may be increasing the recording level of the street traffic noise in the background, the vibration of appliances, or what is known as *room tone* or hum.

Stop and listen to all the sounds in the room where you are now. Even though it might be quiet, you will begin to notice sounds such as the soft whirring of the heating unit, or the humming of your computer monitor. Our brains are able to ignore most of these natural sounds and focus on important audio such as your interviewee's voice. However, cameras will not distinguish between these separate audio sources. If we increase the recording level of a microphone that has been placed far away from the audio source, we will increase the recording level of the room's ambient noise as well.

Signal and noise. When recording audio, we want to increase our *signal* (our intended audio source) and decrease the *noise* (all other sounds in the environment). As we move our microphone closer to the audio source, the audio intensity of our signal will increase exponentially. This will allow us to reduce our gain, or recording level. When we decrease our recording level, we will also decrease recording of all other noise.

Wireless versus wired lavs. Lavalier microphones come in wired and wireless varieties. There are benefits and drawbacks to using each kind of lavalier microphone.

Wireless lav microphones come in two parts: the transmitter and the receiver. The microphone is clipped to the subject and is run into the transmitter. The transmitter then sends an audio signal over radio frequencies to the transmitter. The transmitter is attached to the camera and sends the audio signal into the camera for recording. Wireless lavaliers allow great flexibility for the shooter because the subject and camera are not tethered. However, the radio

Figure 4.5

Boom poles can be used to move shotgun microphones closer to the audio source.

signal between the transmitter and receiver can be disturbed by cellphone, Wi-Fi, or other signals.

Wired lavalier microphones only come in one part. The microphone plugs directly into the camera. Wired lavalier microphones are best used in sit-down interview situations where the subject will not be moving. The upside of wired microphones is that their signals tend to be clean and uninterrupted and there is less chance of recording failure.

Audio meters. Recording proper audio levels is as important, if not more so, than getting proper exposure in your images. Most cameras feature audio meters on the LCD screen or viewfinder. These meters move up and down, depending on the intensity of the audio source and the recording level.

Audio meters give shooters visual confirmation of the loudness of the audio being recorded. However, they do not give any indicator of what sounds you are recording. Be sure to always wear headphones when shooting to guarantee that you are recording your intended source. Without head-phones, for example, you may not realize that you are recording traffic noise rather than your source's voice. If your camera features audio meters, you must be sure to monitor them constantly. Audio meters are similar to zebra lines for exposure, and they will help you to achieve a clean, strong audio signal.

Some cameras feature audio meters with a –12db marker. This is the ideal level for your audio recording to peak, or max out. The –12db marker will show you how high to set your camera's audio gain. If you record audio above this level, you may run the risk of experiencing *overmodulation* or dis-tortion of your audio. This will result in unusable sound. Audio that is recorded below the –12db marker can be salvaged in post-production. If the audio meters on your camera do not have any numbered markers (this is common), try to get your audio levels to record approximately two-thirds of the way up the meter.

As you record, you will notice that the audio meters jump up and down throughout your recording. They do not stay fixed at –12db. The goal is to get most of your audio to jump up and down near, but not much above, –12db. For example, when your interviewees talk, the audio will go up and down to match their speech patterns. When they pause, the recording will drop close to zero. The goal is to keep the meters at around –12db when they are speaking. There may be points where the audio is suddenly louder (for example, your interviewee may get excited talking about a topic) but if the meter is generally around –12db or two-thirds of the way up the meter, then you are getting a good signal. Be sure to check your meters constantly.

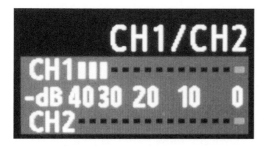

Figure 4.6a
The camera's audio meter is indicating that the recording level is too low.

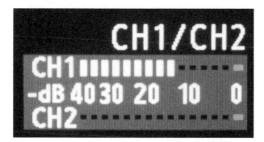

Figure 4.6b
The camera's audio meter is indicating that the recording level is at the correct level.

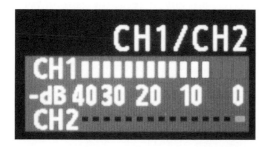

Figure 4.6c
The camera's audio meter is indicating that the recording level is too high.

MICROPHONE PLACEMENT

Understanding the pick up pattern of your microphone and the inverse-square law will help you to better understand where to properly place your microphones. When you are shooting video without the aid of a sound recordist, it often becomes necessary to mount the shotgun microphone onto the camera. This is convenient because you will not need to use a boom poll or other accessories. However, having the shotgun on the camera will require you to get physically closer to your audio source to ensure that you are recording a high-quality audio signal. You cannot stand far away from your subject without picking up all the ambient noise between you and the audio source. As discussed earlier, inverse-square law states that audio intensity is increased exponentially as the microphone is moved closer to the audio source.

In Chapter 3, I recommended that shooters get as many close up shots as possible. To get close ups, videographers should physically move the camera closer to the subject, rather than zoom. Zooming will magnify all your camera moves, and will make your footage appear shakier. More importantly, audio quality also benefits greatly when you physically move closer to your subject. If your camera is closer to the audio source, your shotgun microphone will be able to pick up a stronger audio signal and you will be able to avoid unwanted noise. Shotguns work best when they are less than 5 feet away from the audio source. You can increase the gain on your camera if you are farther than 5 feet away from your subject. But always remember that increasing gain increases the recorded volume of all the sounds, including ambient noise, in your shot.

Shotgun microphones can be used to collect ambient audio or vocals such as person-on-the-street interviews. Lavalier microphones are used specifically to capture high-quality vocal audio. Shotgun microphones have a pick up range of up to several feet, but lavalier microphones are designed to work best when they are placed close to your subject. Lavalier microphones should be placed 4 to 6 inches away from your subject's mouth. Placing your lav microphone further away will require you to substantially increase the gain on your camera. This will result in the pick up of ambient noise such as room hum or clothing movement. Clipping your lavalier microphone too close to your source will result in unnaturally boomy or muffled audio.

Figure 4.7a

The microphone is far away from the source and will pick up significant ambient noise.

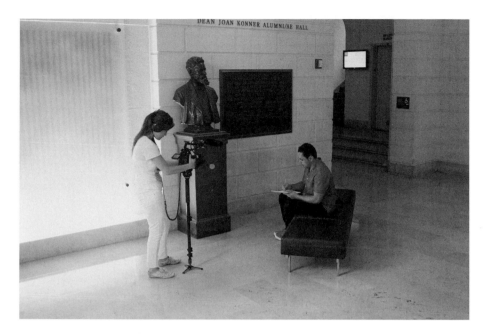

Figure 4.7b
The microphone is closer to the source and will pick up a higher-quality audio signal.

Exercise

Place your camera and shotgun microphone 3 feet away from a constant audio source such as a radio, running water, or city traffic. Adjust your audio gain so that the audio meters are peaking at approximately –12db. Listen to the audio as you record. You should hear a very clean, clear audio signal. Next, move your camera 6 feet away from your audio source. Where do your audio meters read now? How much do you have to increase the audio gain on your camera to reach –12db again? As you increase your gain, do you hear other ambient noise more loudly?

On-camera microphones. Most cameras have a built-in microphone. You should avoid using the on-camera microphone unless you have no other options. These microphones, in general, do not produce high-quality audio:

- *The microphones are not of the highest quality.* Camera manufacturers spend most of their design and manufacturing resources on the camera's sensor, software, and build. Microphones are not generally a high priority.
- *Built-in microphones will pick up handling noise.* Built-in microphones are a physical part of the body of the camera. These microphones will pick up any vibrations on the camera such as your fingers pushing buttons, as well as any mechanical movements inside the camera. These microphones tend to be omnidirectional and are also notorious for picking up too much ambient noise.

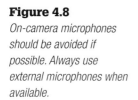

Figure 4.8
On-camera microphones should be avoided if possible. Always use external microphones when available.

- *On-camera microphones are poorly placed*. You cannot adjust the placement of an on-camera microphone. Some manufacturers put their microphones in the center of the camera. Others put the microphone on the left or right side of the camera. The placement of built-in microphones is based on the overall design of the camera, and not on the ideal position for audio recording.

Recording multiple audio sources. Monitoring a single audio source while trying to expose and compose your shots is difficult. This takes intense focus and concentration. Trying to monitor two audio tracks makes your task exponentially more difficult. However, there are situations when you will want to record two audio signals simultaneously. For example, you may want to put a lavalier microphone on a scientist as she is giving you a tour of her lab. You may also want to put a shotgun microphone on your camera to capture the whirring of lab equipment or the chatter of lab workers.

To record multiple audio tracks, you must have a camera equipped with the ability to accept two microphone inputs. Typically, only high-end prosumer to professional cameras will have this capability. Cameras that allow two microphone inputs will allow you to adjust the gain levels of your microphones separately. For example, you may set the recording gain of the lavalier microphone on the scientist at 4. A setting of 4 may be too low for your shotgun microphone and you may want to set that at 6.

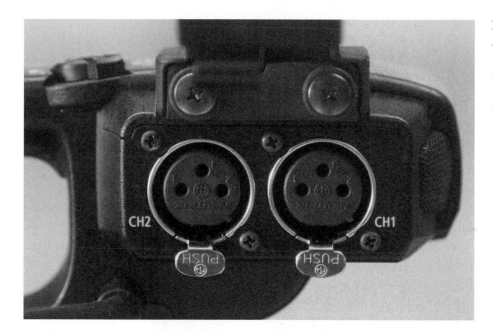

Figure 4.9
XLR inputs are typically featured on high-end cameras, allowing videographers to use high-quality microphones.

After you have adjusted your audio levels for each microphone, it is important to have the camera record each microphone onto a separate audio track. This will allow you to edit each audio track separately in post-production. Refer to your camera's manual for instructions on how to set your recording tracks.

If your camera does not have built-in inputs for more than one microphone, you may want to use an external mixer that will accept multiple audio sources. You can send an audio signal from the mixer into your camera. Using an audio mixer will give you greater control of your audio, but it also adds another layer of complexity.

Tip: If you have the option of recording audio to two separate channels on your camera, here is a trick that protects your audio from becoming overmodulated. When recording a single audio source, set your camera to record this signal to two separate audio channels. Set the audio gain of your second audio channel to record at a level lower than your first audio channel. You will get the same audio recording at different levels on different channels. If your audio becomes too loud in channel 1, the audio in channel 2 will be recorded at a lower level and will not be distorted. You can use the audio in channel 2 if the audio in channel 1 becomes unusable. This works well in situations such as rallies or sporting events when crowd noise is unpredictable.

Figure 4.10

Audio mixers give video producers great control over recording levels and quality.

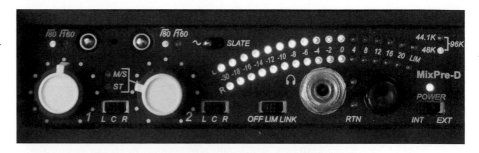

Figure 4.11

Audio mixers allow you to mix channels 1 and 2 separately.

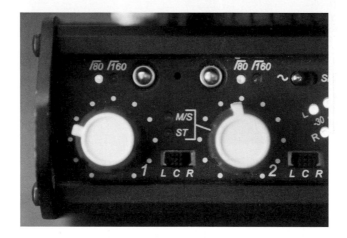

Automatic Gain Control (AGC). Most cameras will offer an option for Auto Gain Control or AGC. Unless you are shooting in extreme situations such as violent weather or unruly protests, you should avoid using the AGC option. Automatic gain control behaves much like auto-exposure on your camera. Software in the camera will try to determine the best recording levels for your audio source. If the audio level is too low, the camera will automatically increase the gain. If the audio level is too high, the camera will decrease the gain. This initially sounds like an ideal solution. However, AGC can produce unwanted results or unusable audio. For example, during an interview, your subject may pause to contemplate a question or he may become emotional and must stop talking. AGC will detect that the audio has gone lower and adjust the gain. We want this moment of quiet, but AGC will begin to record at a higher gain and increase the ambient noise in the room. Conversely, if your audio source is sporadically loud, such as in the case of protest rallies or city traffic, then the AGC will decrease and increase the audio gain quickly and sharply. This will result in audio that fluctuates too quickly and sounds warbled.

Tools for recording audio. Just as there are seemingly many options for cameras and lenses, there are many tools for recording audio. We have discussed using shotgun and lavaliers with your cameras. Often, you will be required to record additional audio with an external audio recorder. External mixers and recorders come in a variety of models, features, sizes, and prices. Some recorders require external microphones, while others have built-in microphones. Smartphones have become great accessories to record audio as well as video. Manufacturers have made microphones and adapters specifically for use with the iPhone to collect and produced audio in the field.

Q&A with the Experts: Sarah Brady Voll, Audio Specialist

Figure 4.12
Sarah Brady Voll, Audio Specialist (holding boom).

What do you do?
I am an audio engineer. When I'm on set, my job is to record the audio so the Director of Photography (DP) can focus on getting the shot. If it's a small shoot, I will mix the lavs and operate the boom. On larger shoots, I am the mixer that monitors all of the different audio feeds. I'm also an audio editor in post-production.

What is the role of audio in a video story?
The picture sets the scene but the sound is what sets the mood. Think about watching a really suspenseful scene in a movie. You can close your eyes and still know when someone is about to get attacked. You can also tell when the

storm is about to end and the sun is going to come out. Every emotion you feel while watching a movie, video, or TV show has been considered and created by the sound supervisor.

*Why can people watch poorly shot video, but they cannot bear
to listen to poorly recorded audio?*

Humans have a tendency to be able to forgive "bad" images. Think about how many times you've watched shaky, out-of-focus smartphone videos. We can watch bad video and fill in the gaps or make mental corrections for bad lighting or shakiness. Our ears have not developed the ability to make these corrections. Static, noise, hard to hear sounds are all difficult to modify in our brains.

What kind of audio gear should all videographers own?

Every videographer needs four things to be able to record sound: a wireless lav, a small directional shotgun mic, a small mixer, and a decent set of headphones. Your on-camera mic is crap.

Why is it better for a videographer to work with an audio field recordist?

If possible, you should always have both a videographer and an audio field recordist. Videographers are very talented people. They know how to set up shots for maximum impact. They can make the most boring rooms come alive by using smart angles and they are dedicated to making the project look as good as possible. Why would you want to interfere with that? Audio adds another layer of complexity that can be alleviated by the presence of an audio recordist.

*What tips you would give any videographer working without
an audio recordist?*

First, know how to use all of your equipment. Don't ignore your microphones and other audio gear. Practice with this gear. Second, record plenty of coverage. Record room tone and fill audio. If you are recording b-roll, you should be recording audio as well.

What is in your gear bag?

My gear kit changes depending on how large and complex the project. My "lightweight" travel kit includes a collapsible internally wired travel boom pole, a Sennheiser 416 shotgun mic, a zeppelin wind screen, a Sound Devices 744T 4-channel recorder, Sony 7506 headphones, four wireless Sennheiser 3G or Lectrosonics with Sanken Cos-11 mics, a Sound Devices Mix-Pre, a Comtek system, a lumbar support harness, a rain poncho, a bunch of high-quality XLR cables, plenty of extra rechargeable batteries for everything, a notebook, a few protein bars, and a bottle of Aleve.

CHAPTER 5

Field Production

WHAT WORKS?

Video has been available online for nearly two decades, but Web technology and users' video consumption habits have changed greatly during that time. The modes of production and the forms of video have also changed greatly. Video is hugely popular online, and it provides a potentially large revenue stream for news publishers. However, there is no current consensus about how news videos should be produced or how they should look and feel. The conventional wisdom of the past was that videos should be short—in the 60- to 90-second range. This mimicked the run times of video packages on local TV. But video online comes in all lengths, styles, and flavors.

Local TV is still a popular source for news, but local TV news viewership is shrinking (similar to newspapers) as more people turn to the Internet as their primary news source. The Web now presents the greatest growth opportunity for video production. I researched and produced the *Video Now* (http://videonow.towcenter.org) report with a team from Columbia University to figure out what worked in terms of online news video. We visited newsrooms such as the *Washington Post*, *The Seattle Times*, *Frontline*, Mashable, and Vice. We interviewed dozens more. We observed their processes, interviewed producers and managers, and we watched many of their videos. After nearly 4 months of research, we came up with some recommendations for producing better online news videos.

1. *Get together. Share ideas.* Video producers need to get together to share ideas. Newspapers, magazines, and broadcasters all have their conventions and conferences. Video news teams and video producers, in general, seem to work in vacuums. There needs to be more collaboration and idea sharing. Many videographers work as freelancers. It is important for video producers to develop a community and to actively engage with each other.

2. *Subject, not medium.* Viewers consume news by subject, not by medium. Audiences do not say: "I want to watch news video." Audiences come

91

Figure 5.1

The Video Now *report (videonow.towcenter.org) features recommendations for producing news video.*

Video Now: Recommendations

online for information on specific topics such as Syria, Ukraine, Obamacare, and sports. Video should be embedded with other media, inside a blog post, or next to a graphic. Videos published with other content get more views. Videos left in segregated video sections get ignored.

3. *Sports and explainers*. Sports and explainer videos did well in every newsroom we visited. Like the old days of print newspapers and TV, people come for sports. Viewers especially love local sports. Audiences also come to be informed about hard-to-understand topics such as economics and health care reform. Both sports and explainer videos consistently got the top number of views in their newsrooms.

4. *Be evergreen*. Breaking news has a short lifecycle, and breaking news videos rarely get re-watched or shared after their initial publication. To get long-tail views—video plays months or years after release— videos should be on topics that have some news value but can have long runs in the news cycle. A specific military firefight may get some views during the news day, but a long-form investigative story on post-traumatic stress disorder (PTSD) may get years of plays.

5. *Long and short*. Videos do not have to be short, but shorter videos tend to get more plays. However, viewers will watch long videos (hour-long documentaries) or an entire series if the content is good enough. Length of video does not predict success, but longer videos need to be well-reported, well-told, and have great production value.

6. *Social engagement*. Video journalists cannot produce a guaranteed viral hit. Most videos never get more than a few thousand views. Instead of

gimmicks such as funny cat videos, news producers need to develop a consistently growing audience. Video producers, whether independent or in newsrooms, should engage new viewers on social media platforms such as Facebook, Instagram, and Vine. Video producers must learn how these and newly launched platforms really work. We will cover ways to promote your work on social media later in this text.

7. *Two teams*. In newsrooms today, there should be two teams of video producers. One set of reporters should shoot fast, raw iPhone clips to accompany their text. These unpolished videos should be posted instantly from the field. The value of these videos lies in the speed of their publication. A second team of highly-trained video journalists should focus on producing in-depth and sophisticated video stories. Avoid the "in-between" stories that are common to local TV news. Stories should be up-to-the-second fast, or deeply important.

It is important to understand how videos are consumed online before you head into the process of producing your video story. While the form and approach of your story may change during the reporting and producing process, you must know what kind of story you are crafting and who your target audience might be. If you are a breaking news reporter, then your video should be fast and raw. Footage coming straight from smartphones feels unpolished but authentic. If you spend time editing your footage, then it may be too late and you will lose the immediacy and value of your raw video clips. If you are looking to produce a longer piece—one that will take you days, weeks, or months—then your story should be worth your production effort and your viewers' time.

FINDING GREAT VIDEO STORIES

As we discussed at the beginning of this book, not all stories should be video stories. Unlike TV, the Internet provides us with the ability to tell stories in various media: quick tweets or updates, long text stories, single photos, slideshows, interactive multimedia projects, and, of course, videos. Journalists must be able to identify which medium and form is the best one for their story. For example, rising interest rates or changing voting patterns across the United States may be best told as interactive graphs or maps. A traffic jam on the local highway may be best told as a tweet. Not all stories command the attention and effort that video requires.

Online, it can be difficult to get viewers to commit to watching a video. From the audience's perspective, it is much easier to read a text story or to look at photos at their own pace. Watching video requires relinquishing control of the speed of the story, and longer stories require a big time commitment from the viewer. Also, in an office or other public setting, video stories require the use of headphones to avoid disturbing co-workers. This is a significant consideration: online news audiences want to consume information with the least amount of time, effort, and resistance.

Motion and emotion. As discussed earlier, motion and emotion are what make a story video-worthy. *Motion* is genuine action. Local TV news often produces what is called *wallpaper,* or footage that provides no new information or fails to advance the story. For example, in a package about rising inflation, local TV news might show footage of shoppers walking through the checkout aisles at nameless grocery stores. The viewer already knows what shopping looks like, and there is nothing in this footage that provides new information.

Emotion is another great value of video. Video allows the viewer to hear directly from the victim of a natural disaster, or the winner of a major sporting event, or the mother looking for her lost child. Video allows viewers to see devastation, joy, and frustration. You must keep *motion and emotion* in mind when you are determining whether a story is video-worthy or whether it can be better told in another medium.

Reporting. As a professor at the Columbia University Graduate School of Journalism, I read many admissions applications. Nearly all of these applications feature essays that declare how much the would-be student wants to "tell stories." Rarely do I come across essays in which the applicant wants to "find stories."

Finding stories is at the heart of journalism. This is the reason why video journalists report, sift through data, visit homes and businesses, and conduct

Figure 5.2

A teacher is working with students in her classroom. This is a good example of active, rather than "wallpaper," footage.

countless interviews, well before they pick up their cameras. I assume that the readers of this book have some reporting knowledge and experience. But it is important to revisit some reporting concepts and discuss how they relate to video storytelling. Too often, new video producers get caught up in the technical challenges of production, and they fail to remember the fundamentals of reporting and storytelling.

Reporting—the gathering of facts, data, ideas, quotes, and other information—is done the same way for a written piece as it is for a video story. The *telling* of a story is where media formats require different considerations and approaches. Reporting does not require a video camera. In most cases, video reporters and producers initially gather facts with just a notebook, pen, or an audio recorder. In video production, this is often called *pre-reporting*. But in actuality, it is just traditional, solid reporting. Reporting is the part of the video production process when a reporter begins to build an idea for a story. It is also the time when video producers must find elements and opportunities to shoot to illustrate their ideas.

Beat reporting. The first step of reporting is to identify your *beat*. Beat reporting is a term that refers to journalism focused on a specific idea or subject. Geographic beats are a common structure for beat reporting. A reporter may cover a community, a district, a town, or a region. Beats can also be topic-based, such as the technology beat or the sports beat. Staying on a beat allows reporters to deeply familiarize themselves with their topic and to build a

Figure 5.3

Traditional pad-and-pen reporting is at the heart of video production.

list of trusted and willing sources. Even general assignment reporters tend to focus on a particular geographic region so they can become highly knowledgeable about that area. It is critical for video producers to establish a beat, and to find sources who are willing to appear on camera.

Sources. Sources are every reporter's lifeline. Sources provide journalists with exclusive information, they help reporters find stories, and they will often introduce journalists to other sources. Sources also help reporters to tell their stories by appearing in on-camera interviews and by giving producers access to their lives. Cultivating a reliable and valuable source list may take months or years. It requires the reporter to genuinely and patiently engage with the individuals and communities in their beats.

Not all sources are humans. Sources can be reports, databases, and other digital information. Learning where to access and find relevant information for your stories requires substantial time and effort.

WHAT IS THE STORY?

Journalists new and old constantly struggle with the question: "What is the story?" Beat reporting and source interviews yield a great amount of information for reporters. However, a collection of facts is not a story. Once reporting has begun and facts have been gathered, the second part of the journalist's job begins—the analysis and distillation of these facts into meaningful stories. Wikipedia is one of the largest resources of information available in the world, but it presents no news stories for readers. A journalist must determine how to analyze and compile reported facts into a meaningful and engaging feature or narrative. But how? Before determining *what* the story is, you must determine *if* it is a story at all.

I have a three-point checklist to determine whether an idea is indeed a story or just a series of facts. If I can conclude that my idea is *new or unique*, then I potentially have a story to produce. If not, I may have to dig deeper in my reporting. These are the questions I ask while reporting to figure out whether I am on the way to finding a good story:

- *Is my story new?* This is the most basic question to ask when identifying news stories. Has my story been told before in another publication or medium? Am I proposing to tell the story in a new or different way? Has the public heard of this before, or is this common knowledge?

  Determining the newness of your story will require Internet and database searches about your story idea. Whether you are producing for yourself or for a publication, you must avoid pitching an old story. There are cases when you can advance an already told story, or

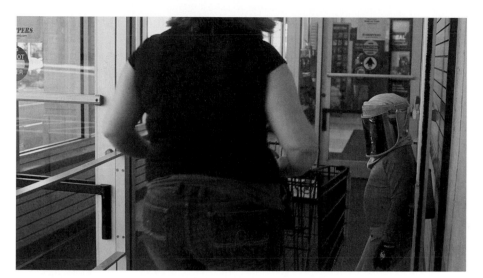

Figure 5.4
Although there had been some print stories about children with extreme sun allergies, there were no video stories about children like Kevin.

tell it in a different way. For example, there might already be a great text story about a new recreational basketball league for veterans recovering from post-traumatic stress disorder (PTSD). You may be able to present this story in a different way by using video.

- *Is there something changing?* Change is often an indicator of whether there is news value in a story. For example, the rezoning of school districts is big news in most communities. The development of a new shopping center is news. Elections and new governments are news. These stories can also be trend stories: new fashion, changing diets, the way consumer habits have developed online. These are all stories about changes, and they often present opportunities for video storytelling.
- *Is there a challenge to the conventional wisdom?* Ideas that contradict conventional wisdom or challenge common beliefs can make for great stories. On local TV news, you will often see stories that challenge old standards: "A new study shows eating fat is not harmful."

New research, new data, and newly disputed facts can lead to in-depth, thought-provoking, and engaging stories. For example, a poor urban community that has long been ruled unsafe, unlawful, and unrecoverable may, in reality, have residents rebuilding their own streets, schools, and businesses with alternative methods and funding sources. Some recent reports about Detroit's bankruptcy have painted the city as a bleak and all but abandoned wasteland. Other reports have come out to show a thriving art and cultural scene in the city. This type of reporting and storytelling requires you to challenge your own ideas and beliefs, no matter how commonplace and accepted they may be.

As you report, ask yourself: Does my story idea meet any of these criteria? If you answered *yes* to any of the three questions above, then you may be on your way to producing a great video news package. If you said *no*, then you should report more deeply. You must find more information or look for a new angle. Otherwise, your set of well-reported facts will never become a story.

PARTS OF A STORY

In this book, we will cover feature, narrative, and mobile video production. While these three forms can be wildly different in approach, tone, and length, they all possess the same fundamental pieces of storytelling: *characters*, *conflicts*, and *solutions* (or attempts at a solution). Video stories must be peppered with facts and data to provide the viewer context, but ultimately, video stories are about people. Interesting video stories are about people with goals, challenges, or problems to overcome.

Characters. When you have an idea for a video story—whether it is a news story, a story about a trend, or a story that challenges conventional wisdom—you must *cast* the best characters for your story. Casting can sound like a Hollywood term used for fiction storytelling, but journalists, especially video journalists, must choose characters for their stories carefully.

Figure 5.5

Matt Atkin, the superintendent of schools and a life-long resident of Piedmont, Alabama, was an ideal subject for a story about education in rural communities.

You must find the right sources to effectively tell your stories. Sources may be great in person or in a phone interview, but they might freeze or stutter in front of a camera. Some sources may grant access to print journalists, while rejecting reporters with cameras and microphones. Some sources may allow you into their homes or offices alone, but they may not have the authority to permit you to shoot in those locations. You must find characters that are informative, are willing to appear on camera, and can give you access to their personal and professional space.

Characters help you tell a story, but they themselves are *not the story*. This statement seems illogical at first, but it is an important tenet of storytelling that we will discuss in greater detail later. Characters provide invaluable information through interviews and access to their lives. But the characters in your story are, in most cases, merely representatives of a larger group. For example, a profile of an unemployed autoworker is really the story about the millions of Americans who were laid off during the recession. You could replace the autoworker with a teacher, police officer, secretary, or any person who is out of work and your story would still be the same.

When producing video packages, you must remember that strong characters are needed to illustrate the facts or points of your story. You must also find sources who work well on-camera. For example, your story topic might focus on technology startups. During reporting, you discover that a growing number of startup companies are being launched and led by women entrepreneurs. This is a valuable news story that shows a changing trend in a certain community. In this case, it is a shift in the technology business world where

Figure 5.6
It took a long period of negotiation and trust-building for Jennifer to allow me to shoot Kevin in their home.

most businesses have been started by men. Your reporting has shown that, in the past year, 25 percent of all new companies were founded by women. That number was only 5 percent during the previous year. Who would you cast to tell this story? And what kind of access will you need from your sources?

The right characters. You must find the right characters to tell your story. While your sources may all have great personal tales of hard work, adversity, and triumph, you must pick the ones best suited for your *specific* story. How will you cast or choose the best sources for your video piece? In the case of the tech startups, you must talk to several new female business owners, their associates, other business owners, academics, and economists. If your story is about the challenges facing this new wave of female tech entrepreneurs, you must find sources going through the process of starting a company. Who can best demonstrate the challenges of raising money, developing products, hiring staff, and taking a product to market? Your best character is one that exemplifies the experiences of the larger trend group.

Interviewing multiple sources ensures that your reporting is journalistically sound, but in video production, it will also ensure that you have characters readily available to be interviewed and appear on camera. Your favorite source may initially agree to be in your story, but she may have to cancel because of a travel obligation. Your second option may get nervous about being on camera or may be told by her investors to wait until another time to participate in your story. Sources will drop out of stories for various reasons. You must have a second, third, or fourth option ready when your first character falls through.

Figure 5.7

Kathie was a perfect character for the film deepsouth. *She was active, articulate, representative, and she gave us great access.*

Enough access. You need as much access as possible to your characters to be able shoot and tell a compelling video story. For a feature or documentary story, you will need to interview your sources several times and to shoot b-roll of them on several occasions. This means that you must go well beyond conducting a single interview. Interviews alone will not give you enough material.

You will need to shoot your sources in action. Will your character allow you to record her business meetings? Will your character allow you to shoot and interview employees? Will your character allow you to have access to her personal life outside of the office? Depending on your angle and approach, you may need to visit and shoot your character several times. Having more access to your characters increases your chance of acquiring the necessary footage to edit your story. If your source does not give you enough access, you may have to find another option.

Comfortable on camera. Being observed or interviewed on camera is a very unnatural event. Some sources will talk openly and articulately to a reporter with a notebook and pen, but they will stutter and find it difficult to speak coherently in front of a camera. Cameras and microphones add a challenging layer of complexity when producing stories. Some sources may be able to provide great information for your story, but, unfortunately, they may not work well as subjects on camera.

In quantum mechanics, there is a theory called the *Heisenberg Uncertainty Principle* that states that particles cannot be observed in their purest state because the force of observation changes the state of the particles.

Figure 5.8
Gaining Jennifer and Kevin's trust to shoot in their home was vital to telling a complete story.

Videographers know this to be true of shooting video as well. By placing a video camera in an environment that usually does not have one in it, the producer has changed that environment. If you film a police officer on his beat, will he act the same way he would without a camera? Would a teacher deal with students the same if she were not being observed? Would a father and child talk as openly to each other as they would when alone? It is impossible to mitigate your influence on your characters and story completely, but you must identify sources who are the most natural and authentic on camera.

How do you avoid choosing the wrong sources for your stories? There are two guidelines that I follow:

- I never shoot anyone who does not want to be on camera. For video stories to be successful, you must have the cooperation of your sources. They must *want* to be on camera. There must be an incentive for your sources to give you open access to their time and their lives.
- I spend as much time with my sources as possible *without* my camera. Pre-reporting and reporting take up the vast majority of my time on a story. Spending time with your characters will allow you to gather facts, assess your sources, and determine your story angle. This period will also give your sources time to assess *you*, your goals, and your motivations. As your sources grow to trust you, your chances of getting deeper access will increase.

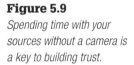

Figure 5.9

Spending time with your sources without a camera is a key to building trust.

Do not profile the first source that agrees to be on camera. Convincing sources to appear on camera, especially in stories about sensitive topics, can be difficult. But you must resist the urge to settle for easy access. While it might turn out that the first person you interview is the best source for your story, this is rare and highly unusual. You must find your story first and then cast the best character to tell that story. If you start with a source and then try to shape your video around that character, you will likely find the process frustrating and unproductive.

Parachuting in. All journalists work on tight deadlines. But despite your time constraints, you must always develop a strong rapport with your sources. This requires spending time developing your beat and building the trust of your sources. Journalists can *parachute* into stories; that is, they can come in for a quick interview and then leave. This will never give you the most meaningful interviews or scenes. In video production, spending a considerable amount of time with your characters in their natural environments is crucial to producing meaningful video stories.

Conflicts and solutions. Once you have chosen the sources to use in your story, you must determine the conflicts your characters face or goals they hope to achieve. This will help you to determine what action to shoot. A common mistake that new videographers make is to use interviews to drive the story. An old adage of journalism is to *show don't tell,* and this is especially important in video journalism. It is the action or the b-roll that you shoot that will move your story forward.

In the female tech entrepreneur story, what are her goals for her company? Goals or challenges that are *specific* are easier to shoot and illustrate than vague ideas or concepts. "To build a successful company" is too abstract of an idea to shoot. How do you shoot "success?" Where do you point your camera and what do you record?

When determining what action to shoot, think of *active verbs* that you can illustrate. For example, the CEO of the tech startup must *raise money* to be successful. How does she do this? Does she present her business plan to potential investors? Does she practice her pitch to her business partners late into the night? Is she producing a video for a Kickstarter campaign? These are all active scenes that can be shot to illustrate her goal of building a successful company. You cannot shoot her "trying to be successful," but you can shoot the many day-to-day things she must do to make her business successful.

Compelling video stories are often about people "overcoming adversity," "defying the odds," or "rising to the challenge." These clichés are, unfortunately, not tangible objects or events that we can shoot. As video storytellers, we must *turn clichés into real, visual action.*

Figure 5.10
Kathie from deepsouth *is a great public speaker, but this only came from practicing on the road and in hotel hallways.*

Exercise

How might you illustrate the follow goals or challenges? Name at least three active scenes that could be potential shooting opportunities.

- A restaurant owner must persevere to stay open during a slow economy.
- A politician must work hard to win over a hostile community.
- An athlete must overcome doubts about his ability to win a championship.
- A new farming bill has cut subsidies for farmers. Farmers must figure out how to survive.
- A soldier overcomes the crippling effects of PTSD.

If these were your stories, what scenes would you shoot to effectively illustrate each goal or problem?

Very often, your video story needs to be completed on a deadline that does not match the timeline of your characters. It may take the CEO of the tech startup years to establish a successful company. You do not have years to follow her story, nor will you likely want to. However, you must show the *solution* or *resolution* to your character's goal to tell a complete story.

To resolve your story, you must look for opportunities to shoot active scenes that are happening in the present time. The CEO's larger goal of building a successful company can be, for example, demonstrated through her smaller goal of rehearsing sales pitches to her business partners. Does she deliver her pitch clumsily at first? Is she forced to rewrite some of her presentation? Do her business partners

Figure 5.11
Shoot your sources in active situations. Do not rely on interviews to tell your story.

encourage her or do they force her to practice more? Does she eventually master her pitch and impress an investor or client? When you present a goal in a story, your viewer will want to know the results of your character's effort.

Profiling sources. Video stories can be, and often are, in-depth profiles of your sources or characters. Stories, especially video stories, are best told through people and their actions. Concepts such as unemployment, the housing crisis, education reform, and universal healthcare can be overwhelming, vague, or confusing to the public. Using relatable characters helps viewers to make connections to these larger issues.

Deciding which sources to profile can be difficult. As we go about reporting, we often grow emotionally attached to many of our sources, even if they are not the best vehicles for telling our stories. We can become impressed by their goals, struggles, and accomplishments. However, this does not mean that these sources are worthy of their own video profile. Sources can provide invaluable information and may appear in our videos in interviews and short scenes. But, to make a source the primary focus of the story, he or she must meet one of two criteria:

- *Representative.* Is your source representative of a larger group of people sharing a common experience that is noteworthy? For example, your source is going through an extended period of unemployment and is having a hard time paying rent and feeding his children. In this case, your source represents the millions of Americans who are also suffering during the recession.

■ *Unique*. Is your source truly unique or *extraordinary*? Has your source won the gubernatorial election? Has she sold her smartphone app for billions of dollars? Has your source cured a terrible disease? For a source to be truly unique, he must have accomplished something that none or very few have been able to do before. Profiles of unique or extraordinary sources are much rarer than profiles of sources who represent a larger group of people.

In a segment on the rising number of homeless families in Florida, the CBS news program *60 Minutes* profiled a brother and sister who were living with their father in a van (www.youtube.com/watch?v=L2hzRPLVSm4). The program follows the siblings throughout the day. In the morning, they wake up and brush their teeth at gas stations. Then they go to school like other kids. At night, they stay at the library until it closes so they can use the computers and read. For fun, they participate in a community theater musical. This gripping, emotional story features these siblings as *representatives* of the millions of people in Florida trying to survive through a crippling recession.

In 2013, ESPN profiled Richie Parker, a designer for Hendrik Motorsports (www.youtube.com/watch?v=qiLDMBDPCEY). Hendrik is one of the most successful racing organizations on the NASCAR circuit. At first, neither Parker nor his story seem to be especially unique or special. However, we soon learn that Richie was born without arms, and he has been navigating life with just his feet and his spirit for problem solving. The video shows Parker learning to ride a modified bicycle as a young child. We see him driving a car with a steering wheel at his feet. We see him deftly using his toes to manipulate a

Figure 5.12

Only one in a million people are affected by diseases such as XP. Sufferers can become deathly ill from exposure to the sun.

computer mouse to design racecars. Richie is not representative of others. He is *extraordinary*, and warrants a video profile. Throughout his life, he has engineered ways to overcome his handicap, eventually landing at the premiere NASCAR racing team.

During the production of *deepsouth*, a feature-length documentary about the rise of HIV and AIDS in the southern United States, over 400 sources were interviewed. Lisa Biagiotti, the film's director, traveled tens of thousands of miles from Chicago to North Carolina and through the Delta to find characters for the film. She researched and reported the story for nearly a year before I joined the project as a producer and the film's director of photography. Her reporting all happened *without a camera*.

From those 400 sources, Lisa and I had to find the best characters to tell a very complicated story. What had caused the rise of HIV/AIDS, a disease that so many had thought to be contained? How were those infected being affected by the communities in which they lived? How were people reacting and responding to the resurgence of the disease? There were volumes of data in Biagiotti's reporting, but to produce the film, we needed real, live people to illustrate and to *humanize* this information. Each of the characters we eventually chose to feature were individually remarkable, but they truly represented a larger community of HIV/AIDS survivors and activists.

Figure 5.13

Director Lisa Biagiotti shooting during the production of deepsouth.

Figure 5.14
A candle lighting ceremony for victims of AIDS.

Unfortunately, in most cases, the sources you meet while reporting will not be representative or unique enough to be profile-worthy. These sources may be able to give you important information, data, and context, but they may not be reflective of a larger group or trend. Your sources may be interesting, but they are likely not extraordinary enough to merit a video profile. Be careful in choosing your sources for profiles.

WORKING WITH SOURCES

The relationship between reporters and sources can be both fruitful and challenging. A reporter must be honest, discreet, charming, aggressive, respectful, and focused when dealing with sources. There will be many situations when reporters and sources must be antagonistic. But, in most cases, working with sources requires sensitivity and finesse, especially when you are wielding intimidating camera equipment. Additionally, as a reporter, it is critical that you do not become too intimate with your sources as to prevent you from producing a fair story.

Incentivizing your sources. A large part of reporting and storytelling requires convincing your sources to participate in your story. In some situations, the publicity and the thrill of being in the media will be enough to encourage your sources to appear in your videos. But, in most cases, you will have to incentivize your sources to give up their time and privacy to you.

Reporters get much from their sources—information, insights, leads to more sources and stories, and access to their lives and experiences. What do sources get from reporters? When I was producing *deepsouth*, it was very difficult

Figure 5.15a
I spent several months shooting Josh for deepsouth.

Figure 5.15b
I spent an entire day in the car with Kathie to illustrate her life on the road.

to convince our sources to speak on camera. In areas like the Mississippi Delta, being gay and having AIDS is still taboo. In some cases, coming out publicly about being homosexual can result in threats or physical assaults. Participating in the film could have put our sources in real danger. We had to find ways to convince our sources to appear in the film.

In *deepsouth*, the characters were different from each other, and it took different incentives to get each of them to participate. Josh was a young man with HIV, and we convinced him that being in the film would show other young, Southern men living with HIV/AIDS that they were not alone. Kathie is an

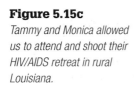

Figure 5.15c

Tammy and Monica allowed us to attend and shoot their HIV/AIDS retreat in rural Louisiana.

HIV/AIDS activist, and we convinced her that the film might be helpful to her fundraising efforts. Tammy and Monica are best friends who run an HIV/AIDS non-profit organization. They saw the film as a way to bring attention to the problems those living with HIV/AIDS face in Louisiana. You must find ways to convince your sources that granting you access to their lives will be worthwhile for them, too.

Deals and negotiations. In video production, especially documentary production, you must ask a lot from your sources. They will give you their time and access to intimate moments and information. Some sources may ask you for money in exchange for access. News organizations have very clear guidelines regarding payment or compensation of sources. Sources may also ask for non-monetary favors or editorial control in the film. How do you handle these situations? These are the guidelines I use for my work:

- *Never give raw footage to your sources.* I never give sources access to my raw footage. Your unedited footage is your visual notebook. Notes should be kept private to protect you, your sources, and other characters. Some sources may back out of your story after they have seen early footage. They may want to censor scenes before you have had a chance to edit your story. Even worse, you run the risk of revealing confidential information about other sources by releasing raw material.
- *Never give your sources any editorial control.* This may seem obvious, but I never negotiate the final cut of the story with my characters. Some sources will not allow you to shoot without granting them some editorial control. If this is the case, you must either incentivize your source to

participate in the story without restrictions, or you must move on to another source. Giving your sources even the slightest editorial control jeopardizes the integrity of your story and your reputation as a journalist.

■ *Never make promises about the angle or viewpoint of your story.* Resist any urges to give hints or make promises about how you will shape your story. During the course of reporting and editing, you will often have to adjust or modify your story. You will discover new information, or you may abandon your first source in favor of another source. You cannot assure your sources how your story will turn out because you yourself will not know until it has been edited.

■ *Be skeptical.* All sources have agendas. When you are negotiating with your sources to participate in your video, you may already be playing off of these agendas ("This video will give your organization great exposure."), but be mindful that your sources will present facts in ways that best promote their needs and interests. They may not necessarily provide you with the most important or meaningful information for your story. Interview your sources, but verify your reporting by talking to several other people. Always bring a healthy amount of skepticism when producing and fact-check your sources.

■ *Never give your sources money for their story.* While it is important to incentivize sources to participate, I never pay sources in cash or in-kind for their involvement in a story. Paying for access has long been a journalistic sin, and for good reason. You must question the motivations of any source that asks for compensation. Are they honest and trustworthy? Are they giving you access because they feel the story is important? Are they simply driven by payment?

Figure 5.16
I bought Kevin and his mother dinner and dessert several times during my time with them.

What about dinner and drinks? I will, on occasion, buy my sources lunch or dinner. I may also have a drink with a source and buy a round. Some news organizations and journalists may frown upon this, but when I am building relationships with my sources, I find that sharing a meal or chatting over a drink is a good way to build trust and intimacy with my sources.

BUILDING TRUST AND YOUR REPUTATION

Gaining access to shoot interviews and scenes requires building trust with your sources. As you develop your beat and journalistic reputation, it will be important for you to be able to come back to sources often. Your sources and audience must see you as an ethical, hard-working, and trustworthy video producer. Here are strategies for building your reputation:

- *Never misrepresent.* These days, it is very easy for your sources to report *on you*. A Google search will quickly show the work you have completed in the past, what experience you have, what kinds of stories you tend to do, and the ways in which you produce those stories. Be honest about your approach and style when you are negotiating access with your sources.
- *Never over-promise.* It is both impossible and inappropriate for you to promise to your sources how your final piece will appear and what impact or reach it will have. Your video may get a million views or it may get 500. Politicians may feel for your sources and pass new legislation, or they may dismiss the video altogether. When negotiating access with your sources, all you can promise is to approach your story with fairness.
- *Always show up on time.* Your sources, like you, are busy people. Respect their time. Show up for interviews and other shoots prepared and on time. Be early if you can be. Make sure you have all your equipment ready to go. If you repeatedly show up late or cancel shoots, you will quickly lose the respect of your sources and access to their stories.
- *Be insistent/consistent.* Show up to your beat often. If you are trying to gain access to a story in a neighborhood, you must spend time in that community, introduce yourself to people in that neighborhood, and show up to community meetings *repeatedly*. This may require months or years of effort. Sources can differentiate the parachuting journalists from those who are committed to telling an in-depth story. Follow up with your sources often, even after you have completed production on your video.
- *Be fair.* Fairness is a highly subjective term. What does *fair* mean and when are you being *fair enough*? This is one of the greatest and most difficult questions to tackle in non-fiction storytelling and journalism.

Your sources do not have to agree with or even like your final story, but they will respect you if they feel you have been fair. But how do you measure fairness? One question I always ask myself as I am producing, shooting, and editing is: *Would I be able to watch this story with my source at my side?* If I have been fair to my sources in the story, then I can comfortably watch the video in their presence. If I have made unfair misrepresentations or factual errors, I will likely want to avoid my sources after the story has been published. Your personal code of ethics is ultimately your best barometer of fairness.

ETHICS

Ethics is, rightly, a large concern for journalists in all media, not just video. At the Columbia Graduate School of Journalism, we require all of our students to take a separate course in ethics to go along with the ethical discussions in each of their other classes. Journalists must adhere to ethical rules of conduct or they risk losing credibility and the trust of the public.

How do video journalists tackle practical questions such as:

> How much can I clean up quotes?
> Can I accept gifts, even small presents?
> How much audio editing and color correcting is within ethical limits?
> How much staging is acceptable?
> Does the use of music affect my story?

The answers to these questions may seem clear and evident, but there are always real-world situations that make these issues less black-and-white. For example, accepting cash and gifts is typically prohibited or frowned upon by journalists. But what if you are reporting in an environment and culture where it is offensive to reject your host's gifts? Rejecting the gift may mean losing access to that source. Staging, or manipulating scenes, can also be considered unethical by journalists. However, historical and crime scene reenactments are used regularly in documentary films. Is it unethical for you to ask a scientist to come to work on her day off so you can shoot b-roll? Journalists have many places to turn to for guidelines to tackle tough ethical issues:

- *Publication's standards.* The publication you are producing for will likely have their own ethics and practices guidelines. Ask for these prior to shooting so that you have a clear sense as to what is acceptable and what is off-limits for your specific publication. Ethics and practices guidelines may vary from organization to organization.
- *Professional standards.* There are many news organizations such as the Society of Professional Journalists (SPJ) and the National Press

Photographers Association (NPPA) and others that have published standards of ethics. If you are a freelancer or producing an independent video, these guidelines will help you in lieu of specific publication rules.

- *Personal standards.* Most of the time, you will have to rely on your instincts and personal standards. Your personal standards may conflict with publication and professional standards and you must ultimately decide how you act in individual situations. Some of these issues may be less critical. For example, your publication may allow you to accept free DVDs or other gifts from movie studios while you are producing a story about Hollywood directors. Your personal standard may be to reject *all* gifts. This may require you to spend your own money to purchase DVDs, but, ultimately, you will feel more comfortable about your actions.

  There will be much harder ethical decisions to make in the field. Perhaps you are producing a documentary on homeless street kids. They are visibly ill and malnourished. Professional standards prohibit you from giving any cash or gifts to your sources. Will you buy food or water for these kids? Your personal ethical guidelines may trump professional standards in this case.

- *Personal prejudices.* It is important for video journalists to recognize their own privileges and prejudices before entering into reporting and producing. Do you have an agenda for your story even before you have begun reporting? Do your conservative political leanings make it hard or impossible to interview Democrats fairly? Does your upper middle-class background make it difficult for you to understand the causes of poverty? Journalists can never completely escape or mitigate their personal prejudices, but it is important for you to determine what yours are and how they can affect your story.

- *Intention.* My personal barometer for ethical behavior is my *intention*. In the course of producing video stories, I may use music to create a mood. I may recreate a scene for my film because there is no existing footage of that time. I may also accept a gift from a source because it would be culturally insensitive not to do so. These are all real ethical decisions I have had to make in my career. I can strongly defend my actions in all these situations because, in each case, it was not my *intention* to alter the story or to deceive my viewers. During situations when you must make ethical decisions, consider the reasons for your choices. Be sure that your decisions never conflict with your ability to tell a fair and honest story.

GETTING READY TO SHOOT

You have done your reporting. You have found your characters. Now, you must get in the field to shoot. Here is a checklist to prepare you to shoot the interviews and scenes needed to tell your story.

Figure 5.17
Videographers must learn to use different cameras and be ready to use different systems.

Right tools for the job. In the past few years, manufacturers have developed a wide range of high-quality and inexpensive tools for producing video. iPhones can now shoot broadcast- and cinema-quality video. Years ago, this would have required cameras costing in the tens of thousands of dollars.

Video producers have many gear options to choose from, but you must consider three important factors when putting together your gear kit: budget, shooting locations and conditions, and visual and editorial goals. There is no single camera or tool kit that is perfect for every situation.

- *Maximizing your budget.* On every shoot, at the very minimum, you will need a camera, a lens, a shotgun microphone, a lavalier microphone, a tripod, and accessories such as extra batteries and media such as SD cards. If you are on a limited budget, you must prioritize your gear list.

  I recommend that you always spend most of your budget on lenses and microphones. New cameras are released often, and camera bodies age and lose value quickly. You can use the same lens your entire career. This is also true of high-quality microphones. In fact, vintage lenses and microphones can continue to hold or increase their value for decades. Remember, it is the lens that makes the image in your footage and it is the microphone that produces the vibrations that get recorded on your camera.

- *Shooting locations and conditions.* Where you shoot and your shooting conditions should also dictate what gear you use. Will you have to be discreet? This will require using a smaller camera such as a DSLR.

Figure 5.18
We used the 5D Mark II and L-Series Canon lenses for deepsouth.

Will you have to upload footage immediately from the field? This will require a smartphone with an Internet connection. Will this be for broadcast? You may have to shoot on a camera that uses a specific codec. Will you be traveling? If so, you may have to pack very minimally. You may have to bring a camera but not a lighting kit, as checking your equipment may incur substantial airline fees. Will you be in hostile environments that require a lot of fast shooting that draws very little attention? You may have to use a small, prosumer video camera with automatic settings. These are all important factors when deciding on your gear kit.

■ *Visual goals*. What do you want your film or video to look like? Do you want it to look cinematic? If so, you will need a camera with a big sensor and lenses with wide apertures. Do you want your footage to look more like TV news? Then you may need to shoot at 30 frames per second on a smaller sensor camera. Do you want footage from the point-of-view of your character? If so, you may need to use a GoPro or other action camera. Determine the look and feel that you want to achieve with your footage *before* you decide on the gear to use.

Picking the right camera. As mentioned earlier, camera manufacturers update and release video cameras regularly. Technological improvements are constantly being made to the camera's sensor, codecs, and overall construction. Between the time this book is written and published, several new cameras will have already appeared on the market.

The following is a comparison of various styles of video cameras (not specific models) and the benefits and drawbacks of using each one.

- *Large sensor video camera*. Large sensor cameras have been specifically designed to capture high-quality video and audio in a form factor that is ergonomic and comfortable for various shooting situations. Their large sensors produce clean images in low light and cinematic-quality footage with extremely shallow depth-of-field.

  Pros: Large sensor video cameras typically feature professional video features such as zebras, peaking, ND filters, a high-quality video codec, professional audio inputs and meters, and a high-quality LCD screen or viewfinder for monitoring footage. These cameras look very robust and professional, and this may help you to appear more authoritative while shooting in the field. Lenses are interchangeable on these cameras, allowing the shooter to have greater creative control.

  Cons: These cameras are generally the most expensive ones on the market. They can be sold as body-only, and you may be required to buy additional accessories such as lenses and shotgun microphones.

Figure 5.19
A behind-the-scenes shot of me shooting on the Canon C100, a Super 35mm sensor camera.

They are larger than other cameras and can be intimidating to some sources. In situations where you require discretion, the professional look of these cameras may work to a disadvantage.

- *Hybrid photo/video camera.* Several years ago, documentarians began to shoot video on DSLR cameras that had been designed primarily to shoot still photos. Today, nearly all still cameras feature advanced video features and have become powerful filmmaking tools.

  Pros: Hybrid photo/video cameras can be a very attractive option for documentarians and videographers. They are a fraction of the cost of large sensor video cameras, but still feature large sensors and great low light performance. They are compact and are great for situations when you need to travel lightly or be discreet. Like the large sensor video cameras, lenses are interchangeable on these cameras. Additionally, hybrid cameras take high-quality still images, a valuable feature that often gets ignored.

  Cons: The ergonomics of hybrid cameras are better suited for still photography than for shooting video. With some exceptions, hybrid photo/video cameras lack professional-quality microphone inputs, audio controls, ND filters, and zebras. You will also have to purchase a separate microphone because the on-camera microphones are generally of very low-quality.

Figure 5.20

DSLRs are a popular option for capturing high-quality video.

- *Small sensor consumer camera.* Small sensor consumer cameras are popular with amateur videographers who want more advanced video recording features than are available on their smartphones. These cameras are compact and were designed for quick-and-easy videography. While lacking many professional features, these cameras can also be powerful tools for video producers.

  Pros: Consumer cameras are relatively cheap, but they can shoot very high-quality video. Their compact size makes them easy to mount in cars and other locations for unique shots. Because they are amateur in appearance, these cameras will draw much less attention to the shooter, especially in environments hostile to the media. In some situations, a more professional video camera or DSLR may be prohibited altogether.

  Cons: These cameras use small sensors, which results in poor low light performance and a very long depth-of-field. They often lack professional-quality audio inputs and controls. Lenses are not typically interchangeable, and this can limit the creative control of the shooter.

- *Sports/action cameras.* Cameras such as the GoPro were originally designed to capture point-of-view video of extreme sports. They have become popular second and third cameras on high-action shoots and productions that require multiple camera angles.

Figure 5.21

Low-cost camcorders are great for situations that require discretion.

Figure 5.22

GoPro and other action cameras can be mounted in tight spaces, on cars, and on drones for aerial videography.

Pros: Sports and action cameras are compact, can be mounted anywhere, and are water-resistant and durable. There are very few features on these cameras beyond a start/stop record button. These cameras shoot very long depth-of-field images. This ensures that your footage will be in focus, even if you are not monitoring each camera.

Cons: These cameras operate in almost all-automatic mode. You just have to hit record. This reduces the creative control you have on your images. Also, cameras like the GoPro Hero have a very distinctive ultra-wide angle or fisheye look that may not be suitable for your production.

■ *Smartphones*. The iPhone and other smartphones are used to shoot more photos and videos than any other cameras in the world. Their ubiquity and ease of use have made them very popular for both amateurs and professional videographers.

Pros: There is a popular saying in photography and videography: "The best camera is the one that is on you." This explains why the iPhone and other smartphones have become the most used camera in the history of photography. They are always present and available, and shoot high-quality footage. Most importantly, they are Web-enabled, allowing for immediate uploads to video and photo sharing sites and servers.

Cons: Smartphones were designed as quick-and-easy video recording tools. There are no manual buttons or controls on the camera, and

Figure 5.23
iPhones continue to grow in popularity as a video news gathering tool.

the built-in microphone will not produce great audio on video shoots. In the mobile video section, we will discuss how to turn your iPhone into a professional video and audio recording tool.

Release forms. When shooting a documentary or a short feature video, you may need to get each of your sources to sign a *release form*, a note that authorizes the use of their likeness and materials in your video story. There are three main types of release forms: Appearance Release, Location Release, and Materials Release. You must bring these forms to your shoots and have the appropriate party sign each one. Lacking release forms may jeopardize the publication of your video later.

- *Appearance release.* Appearance releases authorize video producers to use interviews and other footage in which sources appear. Different versions of these forms will contain specific legal language, but all appearance release forms detail the title of your video, specific shoot dates, and give you full rights to use the likeness and sounds of your sources. Parents or guardians must sign release forms for children under 18.

  Without a signed appearance release, you may have to eliminate your source from your final video. Below is an example of an appearance release form. Be sure to consult with your publisher or legal advisors regarding the specific requirements you will need in the appearance release form for your video project.

Appearance Release

Date: _____

Name of Program: _____

Shooting Location: _____

Shooting Date(s): _____

I hereby agree that _____may record my likeness and voice and incorporate such recordings, in whole or in part, into the Program.

I agree that as between _____ and me, _____ is the sole owner of all rights in the Program, and that _____ has the irrevocable right to edit the Program, use and license others to use any version of the Program and excerpts there from in all manner and media, now known or hereafter devised, worldwide without limitation as to time, including the use of my name, likeness and voice for Program packaging, promotion and publicity purposes.

I expressly release_____, its underwriters, licensees and assigns from any privacy, defamation or other claims I may have arising out of the broadcast, exhibition, publication, promotion and other uses of the Program and the footage containing my appearance therein.

I represent and warrant that I have the legal right and power to grant _____ the rights granted above.

   Accepted and Agreed:

Name: _____

Signature: _____

Parent's Name and Signature (if under 18):

_____

Address: _____

Phone: _____

Email: _____

■ *Location release*. Location releases authorize video producers to shoot in and use footage of a private location. These release forms grant videographers the right to enter and shoot at these locations and to use imagery, including property names and logos, in their video stories. Journalists in the United States may shoot freely in most public locations, but private locations such as homes and businesses require authorization from the owner or executor of those premises. Below is an example of a location release form. Be sure to consult your publisher or legal advisors regarding the specific requirements you will need in your location release form for your video project.

Location Release

Program Title: _____

Production Date(s): _____

Permission is hereby granted to _____ to use the property located at: _____
for the purpose of photographing and recording interview scenes for the above program.

Permission includes the right to bring personnel and equipment onto the property and to remove them after completion of the work. The permission herein granted shall include the right, but not the obligation, to photograph the actual name connected with the premises and to use such name in the Program.

The undersigned hereby gives to _____, its assigns, agents, licensees, affiliates, clients, principals, and representatives the absolute right and permission to copyright, use, exhibit, display, print, reproduce, televise, broadcast and distribute, for any lawful purpose, in whole or in part, through any means without limitation, any scenes containing the above described premises, all without inspection or further consent or approval by the undersigned of the finished product or of the use to which it may be applied.

_____ hereby agrees to hold the undersigned harmless of and free from any and all liability and loss that _____, and/or its agents, may suffer for any reason, except that directly caused by the negligent acts or deliberate misconduct of the owner of the premises or its agents.

The undersigned hereby warrants and represents that the undersigned has full right and authority to solely enter into this agreement concerning the above described premises, and that the undersigned hereby indemnifies and holds _____, and/or its agents, harmless from and against any and all loss, liability, costs, damages or claims of any nature arising from, growing out of, or concerning the use of the above described premises except those directly caused by the negligent acts or deliberate misconduct of _____, or its agents.

By: _____

Signature of Authorized Property Representative

Date: _____

■ *Materials release.* Materials releases authorize video producers to use photos, music, archival footage, and other materials owned by their sources or other parties in your video story. There may be a fee associated with this material, especially archival footage, audio recordings, and photos. Below is an example of a materials release form. Be sure to consult your publisher or legal advisors regarding the specific requirements you will need in your materials release form for your video project.

Materials Release

1. For good and valuable consideration the receipt and adequacy of which is hereby acknowledged, the undersigned agree to furnish the materials described below (collectively "Material") intended to be incorporated in and used in connection with a motion picture ("video") being produced by_____ ("Producer").

   Materials are described as follows:

   _____
   _____

2. I hereby irrevocably grant to Producer the right to incorporate the Material, and any portions or images contained therein, in whole or in part in the Film in any manner at Producer's sole discretion, and to use and exploit the Material in all media, versions and

forms, whether now known or hereafter devised, in all languages, throughout the universe, in perpetuity, including, without limitation, television, the Internet, DVD, books, merchandise and all ancillary exploitation, and in any advertising, publicity or promotion for the Video. Producer has the right to alter or modify the Material in any manner, at its sole discretion.

3. I represent that I have the right to grant to Producer the right to use the Material without the necessity of obtaining the consent of any third person or entity, and that the Material does not infringe the copyright or violate any right of publicity, privacy or any other right of any person or entity.

4. Producer shall have the right to freely assign and license this agreement, and all or a portion of its rights and remedies hereunder, without my consent.

5. Producer may at any time elect not to use the Materials, in which case neither party will have any obligation to the other hereunder.

Agreed and Accepted:

Name: _____

Signature: _____

Date: _____

Phone: _____

Email: _____

Address: _____

_____

Producers are not typically required to obtain release forms for breaking news stories. For example, in a TV news piece about a deadly traffic accident, eyewitnesses do not have to sign a release form to appear in the news package. There is an implied consent and press protections for breaking news stories.

Documentary and feature video producers must have all sources sign appearance release forms. Producers must also obtain all location and materials releases as well. This is especially important if the footage has been shot at private locations. Most networks and Web sites will not distribute documentary videos until all necessary releases have been obtained.

Be sure to get sources to sign release forms *prior* to your first shoot. Collecting release forms after the film has been produced may be difficult or impossible. In some cases, your sources may change their minds and not sign a release form without compensation. In extreme cases, sources may choose to withdraw from your video story. It will be difficult or legally impossible to release your film without obtaining all appropriate release forms.

Location scouting. If time and budget permits, you should do a location scout before shooting. A location scout entails visiting your shoot location to assess any potential video or audio problems. Location scouting will allow you to determine what cameras, microphones, and accessories to bring to your shoot. It will also give you an opportunity, in worst-case situations, to find a different shooting location if necessary. It is costly and time-consuming to schedule a shoot, only to realize too late that you will not be able to use the location you have chosen.

Here are common problems and issues to look for during a location scout:

- *Sound.* Sound is the most important element of video. You must get clean, clear sound that is interrupted as little as possible by ambient noise. This is especially important during interviews.

  During a location scout, check for street traffic and other external noise that may interrupt your shoot. For example, you may want to interview your source at his office. However, the office overlooks a very busy street with cars honking horns constantly. Your microphones will pick up this ambient noise. In this case, you will have to select another

Figure 5.24

Location scouting allow producers to assess any potential shooting or audio problems in advance.

Figure 5.25
Air conditioning and heating units are notorious for ruining interviews.

location for the interview. Also, check for other ambient noise sources such as air conditioning or heating units. Does your source work in an office with loud co-workers? You may have to find a quiet space in the back of the business to conduct your interview.

■ *Light.* Modern cameras provide great low light performance for shooters. ISOs can now go into the tens of thousands. However, some locations such as bars, restaurants, and homes may be too dark even for the newest camera. A location scout will alert you to lighting problems. You may be required to bring external lights to your shoot.

■ *Space.* Will there be enough space at your shooting location to conduct an interview? Is there enough room for your camera, tripod, lights, audio recordist, and your source to all fit comfortably? If not, you may need to find a different place to shoot.

Do you have the proper authority to shoot at this location? Does the building require video crews to enter using a service elevator? A source might invite you to shoot at his place of business, but you might be required to get written permission from the building management. Speak to the appropriate authorities to make sure you are following all proper building protocols.

■ *Shooting outside.* Shooting outdoors and using natural light can produce beautiful footage. It can also present many shooting and production problems. If you choose to shoot at a public park, are you still required to obtain shooting permits? Is it a crowded location with people going in and out of your shot constantly? Is there loud crowd noise? Is there a best time to shoot at that location? Will it be too hot or bright to shoot midday? Scouting outside locations can greatly minimize problems during your shoot.

Figure 5.26
Videographers may be required to bring external lighting on shoots.

Figure 5.27
Some locations may be too small or crowded to shoot interviews or b-roll.

Figure 5.28
When shooting outdoors, be conscious of traffic and other distracting ambient noise.

PRODUCTION

Before you can shoot a single frame of video, you must report, verify facts, vet sources, determine an angle for the story, and select the characters and locations to use in your video. All these tasks are commonly referred to as *pre-production*, or the period *before* you start shooting interviews and b-roll. The more time you spend on pre-production, the smoother your production and post-production time will be.

Once you have completed pre-production, you must come up with a production game plan. A common mistake of new videographers is to go out and shoot too much and without focus. Casting your net widely may work if you are a fisherman, but video producers must learn to produce and shoot efficiently. Shooting unnecessary footage during production will create exponentially more work for you in post-production.

The interview. Interviewing is at the heart of journalism. Interviews are conducted to find facts, confirm information, debunk myths, and, in video storytelling, they are used to narrate and advance your story. Interviews are the editorial backbone of your feature video or documentary film.

There are two equally important concerns for video producers to consider when conducting on-camera interviews:

1. Achieving high production values in both the look and sound of the interview.

2. Acquiring useful information, powerful sound bites, and compelling narrative quotes.

Most factual information will be collected in your pre-production and reporting process. Your source's name, age, occupation, family members, and so on are all background information that is acquired prior to on-camera interviews. On-camera interviews should not be used for this initial reporting. These interviews must be used to record meaningful anecdotes, ideas, thoughts, and quotes that can be used for narration.

Setting up the interview. There are many ways to set up an interview for a video story: studio interviews, field interviews, sit-down interviews, and in-scene interviews. These are all useful approaches, but each will result in a different style. Before setting up your interviews, you must determine how you want your film to look and feel. Your interview style will greatly affect the tone of your entire video piece.

■ *Studio interviews.* Studio interviews are conducted in very controlled environments such as TV studios or soundstages. Lighting is precisely controlled, and ambient noise is eliminated. Backdrops can be installed to create a scene or give the background some visual accents. Studio interviews can feel less vérité and removed from the rest of the action in the video.

Figure 5.29

An interview in a studio setting.

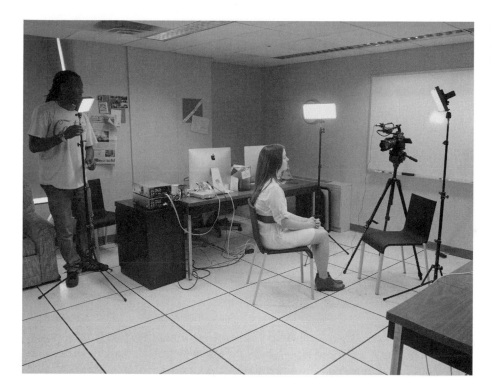

Figure 5.30
An interview in the subject's office.

- *Field interviews.* Field interviews are conducted in real-world locations: restaurants, offices, homes, parks, and so on. These settings are tightly connected to the characters in the video story. For example, a profile of a fisherman might be conducted in the wheelhouse of the boat or on the dock. A scientist may be interviewed in her lab. Field interviews will present more audio and lighting challenges than studio interviews, but they can be visually and editorially important for your story.
- *Sit-down interviews.* Sit-down interviews are the most basic interviewing set up. As the term suggests, this type of interview requires both the reporter and the interviewee to be sitting during the course of the recording. There are many benefits to this technique. Your source is in a fixed position, giving you great control over the framing of the interview. Your subject is comfortable and focused, and this will allow you to conduct a longer interview. Also, *you* are sitting comfortably, and this may greatly reduce your strain and fatigue.
- *In-scene interviews.* In-scene interviews are conducted on-the-go, typically when shooting action. For example, you may be shooting a farmer loading up his truck with vegetables. While he is in action, you may ask him questions about the difficulties of farming or how much he will

Figure 5.31

An in-scene interview conducted while shooting action.

make at the market. The farmer can answer these questions while filling up his truck. In-scene interviews face many technical challenges such as audio, but they can be very compelling and powerful in a film.

Sit-down interviews lack the visceral action of in-scene interviews and can be extremely dull to watch. While most of your footage should be action or b-roll, videographers still must make interviews as visually appealing and dramatic as possible. Interviews provide information to your viewer, and they are also used to narrate or forward the story. They must be well-produced and match the tone of your video.

There are five main considerations for setting up a sit-down interview: environment, positioning, framing, microphone placement, and lighting. Paying careful attention to each of these factors will produce interview footage with high video and audio production value.

- *Environment.* Selecting the best environment for your interview is critical. You must find a location that has low ambient noise. Street traffic, humming appliances, and loud co-workers will result in unusable interviews. You must also reduce visual disruptions in your shot. People walking or working nearby can be terrible distractions to your source and the viewer. The interview location must be big enough to fit your source, your equipment, and yourself comfortably.

  Your interview location must provide some additional editorial value to the viewer. Why are you conducting the interview at this particular

Figure 5.32
When conducting an interview in a public place, be mindful of other people and noise in the background.

location? Does it provide more information or context to the viewer? Would you interview a basketball player in a conference room, at the gym, or in his home? Which makes the most sense for your story?

Resist resorting to clichés when choosing environments for shooting interviews. For example, lawyers will often be interviewed in front of rows of legal textbooks in their office. This kind of shot is dull, lazy, and ineffective. It is likely the viewer already knows that the lawyer has read quite a few law books; the setting and props provide no new information.

- *Positioning.* You must carefully position the camera, your source, and yourself during the interview.

The camera should be at eye-level with your interview subject. Never put the camera above or below the subject's eye-level. If your camera is positioned too high, then you will produce an image that is condescending: the camera and the viewer are looking down on your subject. If the camera is placed too low, then you will shoot up your subject's nose, an unflattering and unnatural angle. It is important that you adjust your tripod for each interview subject to match their height and meet their unique eye lines.

It is important to use a firm, stationary chair or stool for interviews. Chairs that swivel or have wheels will allow the source to move about during the interview. It is critical to keep your source stationary, focused, and in the frame. Overstuffed and soft furniture should also be avoided if possible. Sources may slouch or slide down on a couch or sofa that is not firm.

Figure 5.33

Be sure that the camera is at eye-level with your interviewee.

Figure 5.34

Be sure to use firm, stationery chairs for your interviews.

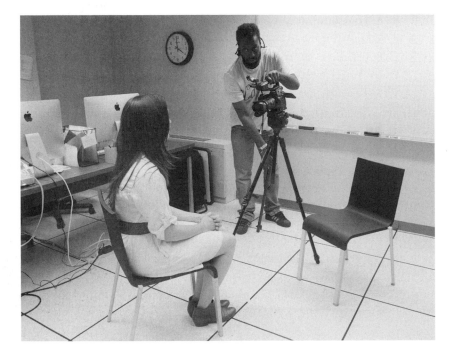

Your sources should never be placed directly against a wall. They should be positioned as far away from the background as possible to achieve the appearance of greater depth and distance in the frame. If the interview location is big enough, you can use selective focus (shallow depth-of-field) to blur out the background to isolate and highlight your source. Make sure that the background is not busy and there are no background objects distracting the viewer from your subject.

Figure 5.35
In this interview, the subject is sharp while the background is blurry.

Figure 5.36
Be sure to remove distracting objects from the background.

During the interview, you should be sitting eye-level and directly across from the subject. Avoid standing during the interview. This will cause the subject to look up, producing an unusual image.

Figure 5.37a

The interviewer should never be higher than the subject.

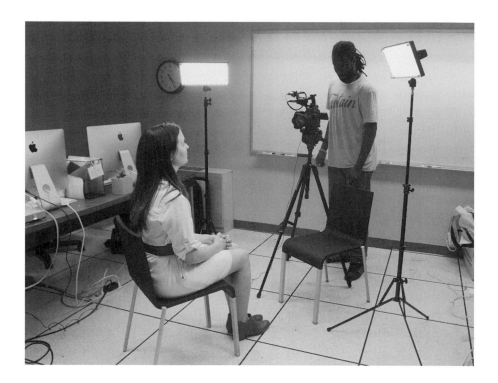

Figure 5.37b

If the interviewer is higher than the subject, the subject will tend to look up during the interview.

■ *Framing.* The most common interview framing technique involves using the *Rule of Thirds.* As discussed in the section on composition techniques, the Rule of Thirds is executed by dividing your frame into nine equal segments with two lines running vertically and two lines running horizontally, similar to a tic-tac-toe board. Rather than centering your interview subject, your source should be placed at one of the top two points of intersection. Be sure *not* to place your subject at the bottom two points of intersection or in the center of the frame. This will make your composition look awkward.

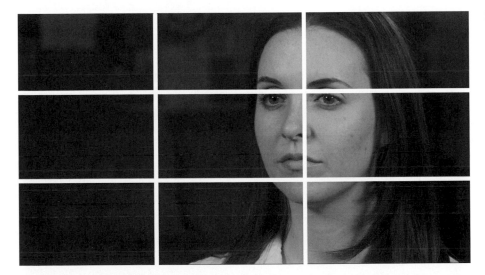

Figure 5.38
Frame your subjects using the Rule of Thirds.

Figure 5.39
Do not put your subject in the center of the frame.

Figure 5.40
Make sure that your subject looks into the frame, rather than out of the frame. This framing is incorrect.

Figure 5.41
Subjects can look off-camera or directly into the camera, depending on your aesthetic choice.

Traditionally, producers have instructed the sources to look at the interviewer, rather than directly into the camera. If you are using this style of framing, make sure that your interviewee looks into the frame, rather than out of the frame. This framing style requires the interviewer to be sitting just left or right of the camera.

Some videographers prefer to have the subject look directly into the camera. This style has been popularized by filmmakers such as Errol Morris and in films such as *The Imposter*. Looking into the camera can create a feeling of deeper intimacy between the subject and the viewer. However, some sources are not comfortable looking into the camera. They may become distracted and look around the room.

Morris uses a special camera set up called the *Interrotron* to keep his sources looking at the camera. If you choose to have your source looking directly at the camera, you have the option of framing him in the center or using the Rule of Thirds as a guideline.

Adjusting the focal length of your shot can create or reduce tension and drama in your interview. Wide-angle and normal-angle lenses result in a moderate distance between the interviewee and the viewer. Telephoto lenses can create images that are very tight and intimate.

Figure 5.42a
Wide interview shots keep the subject at a far distance.

Figure 5.42b
Medium interview shots bring the viewer close to the subject.

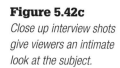

Figure 5.42c

Close up interview shots give viewers an intimate look at the subject.

If it is not distracting to your subject or yourself, adjust your focal length throughout the course of the interview. Your interview framing does not have to be fixed during the interview. Be sure to experiment with different focal lengths before you interview to see what results you can achieve. Stay wider for general questions. Get close ups for intense or dramatic moments. Shooting interviews with multiple focal lengths will result in more editing options later.

■ *Microphone placement.* Audio quality is largely based on three factors: microphone quality, ambient noise, and microphone placement. Shooters should rent or buy the highest quality microphones that they can afford. A good microphone will work for decades. A cheap microphone can eventually cost you more money and headaches in the long run. It is very difficult to fix low-quality audio in post-production.

Eliminating ambient noise is also crucial for your interview. When selecting an interview location, always remember to listen for external audio sources that can interfere with your recording. You cannot delete or scrub out most ambient noise from an audio recording. If your shooting environment becomes too noisy, pause or stop your interview. Do not proceed with your interview with the hopes of fixing the audio problems later. You will not be able to remove this noise. Take a break and resume the interview once the ambient noise has been eliminated.

The microphone should be placed about 5 to 6 inches away from your subject's mouth. If the microphone is placed too close to the mouth, then your audio will be muffled. If the microphone is placed too far

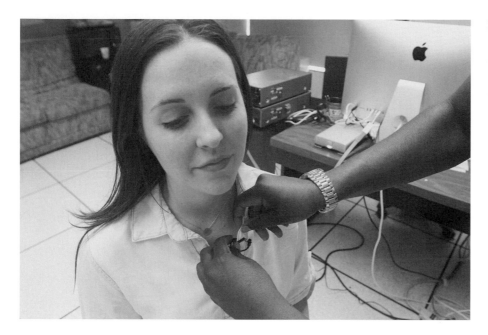

Figure 5.43
Place lav microphones about 5 inches away from the source's mouth to record high-quality audio.

away from the mouth, then you run the risk of capturing a low-quality signal and too much extraneous noise.

Ask the subject to remove any jewelry that may make noise during the interview. Dangling earrings and necklaces are notorious for ruining interviews. Be sure to hide your microphone and cable. Exposed microphones look unprofessional and can pick up unwanted handling noise.

■ *Three-point lighting.* Lighting is truly an art form that can take years to learn and master. Three-point lighting is one of the most basic but effective interview lighting configurations. It is called three-point lighting because three light sources are required to illuminate the interview subject: a key light, a fill or side light, and a back light, also commonly called a *hair light*. You can use various light sources to light your interview: portable LED lights, natural light, and lamps or light fixtures available in your shooting environment.

Lighting serves three basic functions: to provide general illumination to the scene, to highlight specific elements in your frame, and to add depth or texture to your scene. B-roll is typically shot with natural or available light. You must actively light your interviews to highlight your subject and to make this static shot more visually appealing.

Figure 5.44

Three-point lighting is a basic, but powerful, configuration for achieving well-lit interviews.

After you have positioned and framed your interview subject, you can light your shot:

- *Step 1: Control ambient light.* The first step in lighting your interview is to eliminate light sources with conflicting Kelvin temperatures. As discussed earlier, a camera will reproduce accurate colors only when it has been properly white balanced. Mixing different light sources with different color temperatures will result in portions of your shot being too orange and other portions being too blue. For example, if I shoot a scene that is primarily lit with tungsten lamps and my camera has been white balanced for tungsten light, the scene will have accurate colors. However, if there is a window with daylight spilling into the shot in the background, the window and the light around it will appear to be bluish in tint.

  You must take control of the light sources in the interview environment. Cover up windows if you will be lighting with tungsten light sources. Turn off lamps if you will be using daylight-balanced LED lights. If you do not have a blanket or drapes to cover a window, then you must be sure to frame the shot so that the window and any daylight spilling into the room is out of the shot.

- *Step 2: Key light.* Once you have eliminated conflicting light sources, you must set your *key light*. Your key light is, in general, your most powerful light source, and it is used to provide most of the illumination on your subject. Your key light is placed about 30 degrees from your camera in relation to your subject. To avoid shining lights directly into your source's eyes, place lights above the subject, tilting down at about a 30 to 45 degree angle.

Figure 5.45
Be careful not to mix light sources. Daylight coming in the window will appear to be blue compared to the incandescent light in the room.

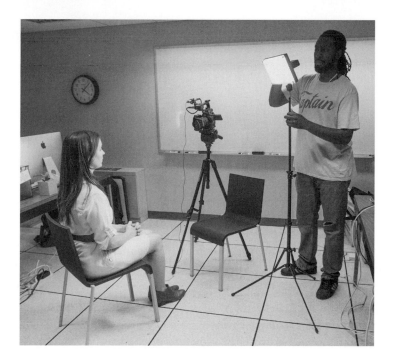

Figure 5.46a
A videographer setting up the key light.

Figure 5.46b

The subject has been lit with only the key light. Note the dramatic shadows on the subject's face.

Figure 5.46c

The subject has been lit with only available light. The image is flat and dull.

Some lighting kits have dimmers to adjust the intensity of the light. Use dimmers to adjust the amount of light on your subject until your subject's face is properly exposed. If your light does not have a dimmer, you must move the light further or closer to your source to adjust the intensity. Like audio, light intensity follows the *Inverse-Square Law*. If you move the light away from the subject, the intensity of the light will decrease exponentially.

A key light will illuminate most of your subject's face and separate it from the background. Compare the two screenshots. The second interview only uses available light and appears to be very flat. The first uses a key light. This shot has much greater depth and the source is separated from the background.

Key lights will illuminate your subject, but notice that it will also leave harsh shadows across his face. Some shooters like this dramatic look and choose to use only a key light. Crime, mystery, and investigative documentaries often use this style to increase tension and suspense.

- *Step 3: Fill light.* The *fill light*, also known as the *side light*, is used to eliminate the shadows created by the key light. Fill lights are placed on the side of the subject that has the shadows. Like the key light, the fill light is typically placed at a 30 to 45 degree angle above the subject.

  By increasing the intensity of the fill light, you will flatten out the lighting on your subject. Experiment with how much fill light you want to use in your shot. Using a little bit of fill light will slightly decrease the shadows on your subject's face. Some faint shadows will remain, preserving some depth and contrast on the face. Increasing the fill light will make the subject more evenly lit. This will eliminate all shadows and will flatten out the subject's face. The intensity of the fill light will have a direct effect on the dramatic effect of the key light.

- *Step 4: Back light.* Many videographers will stop lighting after setting the key and fill lights. Two-point lighting does an excellent job of illuminating the subject, separating the subject from background, and balancing out

Figure 5.47a
A videographer setting up the side light.

Figure 5.47b
The subject has been lit with the key and side lights. Note the even lighting on the subject's face.

Figure 5.48a
The videographer setting up the back (or hair) light.

any harsh shadows that may appear on the subject. Some videographers will choose to use a third light to further highlight their subject.

The *back light*, or *hair light*, is placed behind the subject, but just out of the frame. Like the fill and side light, this light is also placed above the subject, angled down similarly to any ceiling or track lighting

Figure 5.48b
The subject has been lit with the key, side, and back lights. Note that the subject's hair pops from the background.

Figure 5.48c
The subject has been lit without a back light. Note that the subject's hair blends into the background.

you may find in a home or office. The purpose of the back light is to illuminate the subject's hair and shoulder lines just slightly, creating an outline around your subject.

Compare the two screenshots. The second interview does not feature a back light. The first interview features a back light that creates an outline around the subject's head and shoulders. Notice that the subject in the first image appears to be more separated from the background than the subject in the second image.

Figure 5.48d

Be careful not to use too much back light or you may risk "burning" your subject.

Be careful not to use too much intensity in your back light. A back light that is too bright or has been poorly positioned will create unwanted hotspots on your subject.

- *Step 5: Set exposure and white balance.* Once you have set all your lights, you must reset your exposure and white balance. If your camera has zebras, use them as a guide for measuring proper exposure on your subject's face. A properly exposed interview subject will have some zebra lines in the highlight areas. The subject's face should not be covered with zebra lines. This is an indicator that the image is over-exposed. Avoid eliminating all zebra lines from your subject. Without some zebra lines on your subject, you run the risk of under-exposing your shot. As a guide, I allow approximately 10 percent of my subject's face to be covered in zebra lines. Adjust your aperture or ISO settings to achieve proper exposure.

  Before recording, be sure to set your white balance again. Changing the lighting in the scene can often affect the color temperature of your shot. It is best to white balance right before you start your interview.

- *Step 6: Lighting accents.* Additional background lighting can be used to create a more interesting shot. Lamps or accent lights can make your shot more natural, lively, or dramatic. Diffused lighting on a back wall or the use of patterns can make a flat or solid background appear to have texture.

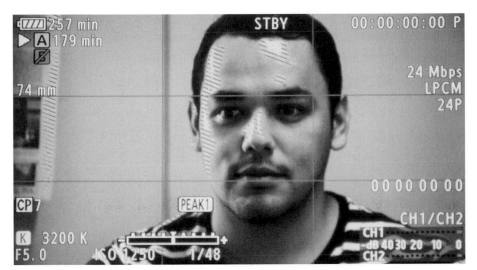

Figure 5.49
This image is properly exposed. There are only a few zebra lines on the subject's face.

Figure 5.50
This image is over-exposed. The image is covered with zebra lines.

Properly lighting an interview scene takes considerable time. With practice, you will become faster and more skilled at setting up lighting. Time yourself to see how long it takes for you to position a two- or three-point lighting set up, and add this to the time you need to interview your subject. For example, if you have an appointment to interview a source at 12 PM and you need an hour to set up your gear and lighting, let your source know. Request to arrive

Figure 5.51

Use background accent lights, such as lamps, to create interesting interview shots.

Figure 5.52

Use splashes of light in the background to create depth in your shot. Note the light reflected off the back drop.

and have access to your interview location at 11 AM. Do not arrive at noon and make your source wait around as you set up. This may frustrate the interviewee, or worse, your subject may have to stop the interview before you have completed your questions.

Tip: If you do not have access to a three-point lighting kit, you can use environmental light to illuminate your subject. For example, windows provide great natural lighting. If the window is directly in front of your subject, he will be evenly lit. If you move the subject to the side of window, he will be lit more dramatically.

Figure 5.53a
Use available light, such as windows, to brighten your subjects. In this shot, the window is in front of the subject.

Figure 5.53b
Use available light, such as windows, to brighten your subjects. In this shot, the window is to the side of the subject.

Exercise
Practice setting up interviews and lighting in at least three different locations. Remember to:

1. Pick a location that will work for video and audio.
2. Properly place the camera, the subject, and you.
3. Frame your subject appropriately in the shot. Try to separate your source as much as possible from the background.
4. Place your microphone in the proper location.

5. Use three-point lighting to accentuate your subject and the interview location.

Ask your subject a couple of questions and record the footage. How long did it take you to set up each interview? What were the biggest challenges of your environments? What were the biggest challenges of three-point lighting?

INTERVIEWING TECHNIQUES

Successfully interviewing a source requires diligent *research and preparation*, *active listening*, and a *clear focus and definition of the goals* of the interview.

Prior to interviewing your source on-camera, you must go through an extensive reporting phase. During your reporting, you will find out important background information about your source: age, full name, occupation, relationship to other sources, relationship to your story, and so on. Ideally, you will have already interviewed your source several times off-camera. Diligent reporting will allow you to form on-camera questions that yield useful answers. During your reporting, you will be able to determine if your source is a good candidate to go on camera. Will he give you open access and be able to answer questions clearly and succinctly? Have other sources confirmed that your interviewee is honest and trustworthy? Is your source an authority on the topic and will he contribute meaningfully to your story?

Do not set up or shoot any on-camera interviews until you answer these questions:

What is the role of the interview? How do you plan to use the interview answers? Will you or someone else narrate the story? Will the interviewee's answers be used as anecdotes, observations, or opinions tied together with your narration? Or will your story be non-narrated? If your story is non-narrated, your subject's answers must provide enough facts, context, anecdotal moments, and narrative descriptions to advance the story in a clear way.

It is much easier to write a script and to narrate your video in post-production. If your sources do not precisely or succinctly answer questions, your narrator can clarify the interviews. Non-narrated stories are challenging, but they can be much more intimate. If you choose to produce a non-narrated story, you must solicit enough strong sound bites and quotes from your sources to be able to tell your story. It is important for you to determine which style of storytelling you will use—narrated or non-narrated—before you begin to shoot your story. You must know if you are getting meaningful answers in your interviews.

Interview check list. Once you are ready to begin your interview, go through this check list to avoid any technical errors during the recording of your interview:

- Make sure your camera's battery has been fully charged and your recording media has been loaded and formatted. Be sure to have extra batteries and media on hand. Every videographer I know has experienced the pain of going to a shoot without enough batteries or media. This is an expensive and easily avoidable error.
- Check that your white balance and exposure settings are correct.
- Clip the lavalier microphone onto your subject and test that the microphone is sending an audio signal to the camera.
- Actively listen for ambient noise. Is the air conditioner on? Your camera will pick up all room and street noise.
- Check your interviewee's audio levels. Make small talk with your source—ask about the weather or the local sports team. As your source speaks, adjust the camera's gain so that your recording meter peaks at around –12db.

CONDUCTING THE INTERVIEW

It is important to put your sources at ease. Being interviewed on camera is unusual and can be a very uncomfortable experience for many people. The term *interview* alone can create feelings of stress. You may want to refer to interviews as chats or conversations to reduce any anxiety for your sources ("I want to chat about how your business is doing."). But always remember that interviews are not normal conversations. Interviews are purposefully conducted to produce clear and useful responses.

Figure 5.54
An interview with the superintendent of schools for a story about technology and education.

Prepare your sources for the interview. In many cases, your sources have not been interviewed on camera before. To make my sources more comfortable, I try to explain as much of the interview process to them as possible. Making the production process transparent can help sources to feel more at ease ("Sorry for all the lights, but they will make the room brighter and make you look great.").

Give your sources a general description of the interview topics, but do not give exact questions in advance. You do not want sources to give answers that have been too rehearsed or prepared. Also, give your interviewee an accurate sense of how long the interview will last. Your source may become agitated or annoyed if the interview lasts for 2 hours when they were expecting to go for 30 minutes.

Warming up your sources. The first question I always ask my source is: "Can you please say and spell your name?" Having your source say her name will help you to pronounce it correctly if you need to narrate the story. It is also good to have the correct spelling of your source's name.

You can ease into the interview with one or two safe questions. "What is your title here, and how long have you been with the company?" You may already know the answers, but these questions can be considered practice swings or warm ups for your source. These questions will give her a chance to get acclimated to the lights, the camera, and you. Do not ask too many basic, fact-finding questions that should have already been asked during your reporting. On-camera interviews should be used to elicit questions that are illustrative, emotional, or provide narrative detail.

Organize your questions. You cannot predict how your sources will answer your questions, but you can keep your line of questions organized and focused. Organize your questions by date and time if you need clear and sequential explanations of events. Organize your questions by themes. For example, when interviewing an entrepreneur, ask all questions about her education and training first, followed by questions about the challenges of running her business. Finish off the interview with questions about her plans for the future of the company. Avoid jumping around too much during your line of questioning. This may confuse your source, and it may also make you forget to ask about important questions.

Good questions get good answers. Repeat and follow up on questions until you get answers that are illustrative, emotional, or provide enough narrative detail. For example, you may be interviewing an entrepreneur for a business story:

> Question: *How challenging is running your own business?*
>
> Interviewee: *It's really hard. It's a big task.*

"It's really hard. It's a big task" is not a useful answer. What does "hard" or "big task" specifically mean? Repeat or modify your question until you elicit a stronger answer. This requires you to actively listen to the responses. Inexperienced reporters will accept weak answers and quickly move on to the next question. You must discipline yourself to focus on both your questions and your source's responses. Push for more specific and meaningful answers:

Question: *Can you be more specific? What are some of the big tasks you deal with?*

Interviewee: *As a startup, I have to do everything myself. I am the accountant, head of HR, CEO, and the cleaning crew. I have to do the spreadsheets and take out the garbage. It's a lot for one person.*

At this point, you have gotten some more specific information about the interviewee's business life. Now you can follow up with a question to elicit a more emotional or descriptive response.

Question: *Describe what that feels like.*

Interviewee: *It can be great, but most days it's frustrating. It feels like I'm out in the ocean and swimming to shore but the tide keeps on pushing me back. There's always more to do.*

"It feels like I'm out in the ocean and swimming to shore, but the tide keeps pushing me back" is a particularly strong quote. It is descriptive, emotional, and is much more meaningful than "It's really hard." Asking open-ended questions such as "Describe what if feels like" will, in most cases, produce strong responses.

During interviews, your sources may go off on tangents that are not useful for your story. For example, while answering questions about working long nights at her startup business, your source may begin to talk about how difficult her professors were in graduate school. Her professors and her graduate school experience are not germane to your story. You must be polite but firm and *redirect* the questioning back to your original points and topics:

Reporter: *Grad school seems really tough. But I have a question about how you came up with your product idea.*

Avoid yes or no questions. When interviewing your subject, avoid asking yes or no questions. An answer of "yes" or "no" is not editorially meaningful and can rarely be used in post-production. Ask your subject open-ended questions that will result in complete answers. For example, "Do you like the President?" can be reworded as "Can you talk about the President's recent performance?" Open-ended questions tend to result in more complete answers. They also provide you with opportunities to refine and repeat your question, or to ask a more direct follow-up.

Figure 5.55
An interview with a student for a story about technology and education.

Exercise

Rewrite these "yes or no" questions. Your new questions should be open-ended to elicit a more specific or meaningful answer.

- Is it hard to own a company?
- Is nursing a rewarding occupation?
- Are you going to vote for this candidate?
- Is education reform important to you?
- Do you feel safe in your neighborhood?

Silence is golden. During our regular conversations, we tend to give audible cues to signal that we are listening and that we understand what is being said. "Uh huh. Yep. Hmmmm." During an interview, you must be silent when the subject is speaking. Any words or sounds that you make will be mixed in with your subject's answers, making them unusable in post-production. When your subject is answering, maintain eye contact. Nod silently or react with facial expressions to signal that you are paying attention. This will help you to maintain a connection with your subject without affecting your audio recording.

Avoid the urge to ask a question immediately after your source has finished the previous one. If you feel that your source has more information even though he has stopped talking, pause for a moment. This awkward silence will often compel your subject to answer the question differently or in greater detail.

Wrapping up. At the end of the interview, always ask your source if you have missed anything or if he has anything else he would like to discuss. This will give your source the opportunity to share new information, direct you to other sources, or to highlight points you did not assume to be important.

Once your interview is over, review a few minutes of your interview footage in the camera to see that your interview was recorded properly. Occasionally, a camera will fail to record footage or the interview will be corrupted. Checking your footage immediately will give you an opportunity to reset the camera and ask your questions again, depending on the availability of your source. While this can be very embarrassing, correcting your mistakes right away is much more efficient and practical than rescheduling an interview.

SHOOTING ACTION

Interviews give information, emotion, and narrative details, but action and motion illustrate and drive your video stories. Just as you prepared carefully to shoot your interviews, you must also prepare to shoot action or b-roll. When you are shooting your stories, you must be specific and precise about the footage that you need to capture. Shooting without a goal or plan will result in many wasted hours.

Should you shoot action or interviews first? In reality, it is best to interview and shoot b-roll of your characters several times. During an interview, your source might mention an exercise routine she does every morning to mentally prepare for her job. This is an *interesting, active detail* about your source. You will want to illustrate this by shooting your interviewee's exercise routine. In this instance, an interview answer has led you to opportunities for shooting action.

After you have watched the footage of her morning regimen, you realize that you need her to explain how each routine helps her perform better at work. You will have to interview your source again, this time asking specific questions about the exercises you have recorded. Here, action has led to another interview.

Avoid wallpaper. Your action shots, or b-roll, should be as editorially meaningful as your interview questions. You must avoid shooting generic b-roll or wallpaper. These generic shots do not add value to your narrative. You must look for opportunities to shoot *genuine* action or motion.

B-roll is used to visually illustrate and demonstrate concepts, behaviors, or ideas. You must be a keen observer and listener to identify active scenes to shoot and include in your stories. You can look for shooting opportunities while you are reporting and while reviewing your interviewee's answers.

Let's return to the earlier example of the CEO of the tech startup. One part of the interview yielded these answers:

Reporter: *What are some challenges of running your own business?*

Interviewee: *It's really hard. It's a big task.*

Reporter: *Can you be more specific? What are some of the big tasks you deal with?*

Interviewee: *As a startup, I have to do everything myself. I am the accountant, head of HR, CEO, and the cleaning crew. I have to do the spreadsheets and take out the garbage. It's a lot for one person.*

Reporter: *Describe what that feels like.*

Interviewee: *It can be great, but most days it's frustrating. It feels like I'm out in the ocean and swimming to shore but the tide keeps on pushing me back. There's always more to do.*

In this case, you want to illustrate the fact that the source faces many challenges as a CEO of a startup. One major challenge is that she must wear many hats and complete tasks that range from high level to menial. What b-roll should you shoot?

The CEO in this story says that her job is "really hard. It's a big task." This does not give us enough practical possibilities to shoot. You cannot point your camera at an object called "a big task" and hit record. "A big task" is only a vague concept. You must find out what your character *specifically* does as a CEO and visually illustrate it.

In her follow-up answer, the source says, "I am an accountant, head of HR, CEO, and the cleaning crew. I have to do the spreadsheets and take out the garbage." Here, we have been given a bit more specificity. What are some of the active scenes she has mentioned? What does it mean to be an accountant? What does it mean to be head of HR? What are her tasks as a CEO? As her own cleaning crew, she takes out the garbage.

You must now decide what to shoot to illustrate your source's responsibilities and struggles as an entrepreneur. Do you want to shoot her acting as an accountant? Is that visual enough? By her own account, this involves dealing with spreadsheets. Someone sitting at a computer typing does not make for very active or exciting footage. What does it mean to be a CEO? Later in the interview, you find out that she works with designers to fabricate her product prototypes with a 3D printer. This is a much more active scene than someone working on a spreadsheet. In this case, to illustrate the "big task" of being a CEO, you might choose to shoot your source working with her designers to develop prototypes.

Shooting scenes. Earlier in this textbook, we discussed the 3 × 3 Rule. This principle requires that you shoot every action from three angles and three focal distances (wide shot, medium shot, and close up). This ensures that you will get a variety of angles and shots. This is a good starting point for shooting b-roll and scenes.

I define a scene as *an action that results in a reaction*. B-roll by itself is not a scene. Shooting complete scenes requires using the 3 × 3 Rule, as well as shooting both *reaction* and *point-of-view (POV)* shots. When you are shooting scenes, make sure that your raw footage, when properly edited, will provide information that fully complements or enhances your interviews.

Five shots. I follow a five-shot formula to ensure that I will have enough material to create a scene in post-production: wide shot, medium shot, close up shot, reaction shot, and point-of-view (POV) shot.

- *Wide shots.* Wide shots provide context to your scene. Wide shots give your viewers a sense of place, the number of characters in your scene, and any other relevant details. For example, in a scene with students, a wide shot will establish that they are in a classroom or lab of some sort. Without a wide shot, the location or setting may be unclear. Wide shots are sometimes referred to as *establishing shots* because they establish the setting.

Figure 5.56
Wide shots provide context to your scene.

- *Medium shots.* Medium shots can help you to focus your scene. In a classroom with many students, a medium shot will allow you to focus on two students in particular. I tend to favor editing with wide and close up shots, but medium shots are invaluable for building a scene.
- *Close ups.* Close ups provide crucial detail to your scene. As a videographer, one of your main goals is to be a surrogate for your viewers. Close ups of people, the objects in the room, and other details will bring your viewers closer into the environment and give them a deeper sense of the scene. In general, approximately 60 percent of the shots I end up using in my videos are close ups.

Figure 5.57

Medium shots help to focus on the primary subjects of your scene.

Figure 5.58

Close up shots provide crucial detail to your scene.

- *Point-of-view (POV)*. A point-of-view shot helps to place your viewer into the story. In your classroom scene, your wide shots provide context and setting, medium shots isolate your main subjects, and close ups present detail. Your POV shot gives your viewers a more intimate view of the scene. POV footage is shot from the vantage point of one of the characters, rather than that of the reporter or observer.
- *Reaction shot*. Wide shots, medium shots, and close ups demonstrate action. To complete a scene, you need to shoot reaction shots. If one student is discussing a project with another student, then we must show

Figure 5.59
POV shots help to place the viewer into the story.

Figure 5.60
Reaction shots demonstrate the impact of the action in the scene.

Figure 5.61

A sequence of wide, medium, close up, POV, and reaction shots form a complete scene.

Figure 5.62

Footage shot from the same angle and edited together will result in a jump cut.

how the student is reacting. If a musician is playing on stage, we need to see the audience. If a politician is speaking, we must see the cheers or boos of the crowd.

Many videographers use a modified version of this five-shot formula. There is no absolute right or wrong formula, but the key point to remember is that you need a variety of shots to be able to edit a real scene with action and reaction. See how the five shots we discussed come together as a complete scene. Even in a very dull environment such as a classroom, you can create motion if you capture enough of the right shots.

Cutaways and transitions. Two other shots that you must be concerned with while shooting in the field are *cutaways* and *transitions*. Cutaways are shots you can use to *cut away* from your action. You will often have to edit footage to make your scene more concise or understandable. This editing may produce *jump cuts* or edits that awkwardly juxtapose shots from similar angles. Jump cuts can be jarring to a viewer.

A cutaway allows you to edit in another shot then go back to your previous angle. Cutaways should be meaningful—always avoid wallpaper. Avoid generic cutaways such as hands typing on keyboards or clocks on walls, unless, of course, the time of day matters to the scene.

Transition shots help you to get from one scene to the next scene smoothly. Establishing shots are often used to get viewers from one location to a new setting. For example, after the scene in the classroom, you may want to transition to a scene that takes place somewhere else on campus. This may be an outside shot of another school building or the campus quad.

Figure 5.63
Cutaway shots (the middle frame) allow editors to return to a previous shot without producing a jump cut.

Figure 5.64
Establishing shots give viewers a sense of place.

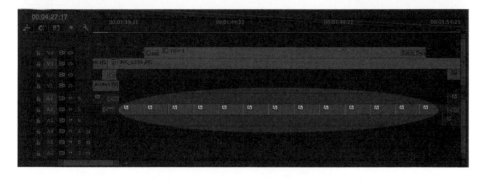

Figure 5.65
Room tone added to a sequence.

Collecting ambient sound. Ambient sound can greatly harm your shot. Street noise, loud machinery, and people talking can all ruin your footage. But ambient noise can be very powerful for drawing your sources into your scene. It can also be vital for sound editing later.

Before your leave any location, identify the noises and sounds that are unique to that environment. If you are shooting at a construction site, be sure to get high-quality recordings of hammers, saws, and other ambient noise specific to that environment. If you are at the ocean, be sure to record sounds of waves hitting the shore. These recordings should be isolated sounds—no talking or other ambient noise. Even if you are in a seemingly silent room, be sure to record a few minutes of *room tone*. This room tone can be used later to layer under audio edits.

Q&A with the Experts: Jason Mojica, Editor-in-Chief, VICE News

Figure 5.66
Jason Mojica, Editor-in-Chief, Vice
Photo: *Zach Goldbaum*

How did you get started in video?

I studied film for about a year as a freshman in college before dropping out. When I went back to school 12 years later, it was to study political science. Ironically, it was studying politics and international affairs that drove me back to film and video because I began to understand the importance of storytelling and mass media in how things play out on the world stage. In 2006, I took an internship at a Washington, DC-based non-profit that was making a reality show designed to bridge the gap between the U.S. and the Arab world and I became more and more convinced that I could have a greater impact on the world through video than by being a policy wonk. At the time, I was struggling to understand why everyone seemed to agree that something had to be done about the crisis in Darfur, yet nobody seemed to be doing anything about it. While drunk at a bar with a couple of friends, we joked that we should just hop on a plane and go there and figure it out and make a film about the process. That's what we did, and that experience forever altered my life. I remember thinking, "Imagine if I could get *paid* to do this!"

What kinds of stories work best for video?

The best stories for video are stories that are happening *right now* . . . stories that are unfolding right in front of your camera. This sounds like a no-brainer, but I mean this in contrast to stories that have happened in the past that people are trying to convey with words. I like stories that are kinetic, where things are *happening*, where I can't believe I'm lucky enough to be there to witness them and share them with an audience.

What three tips would you give videographers in terms of finding and reporting video-worthy stories?

1. Pick stories that have a beginning, middle, and end.
2. Pick stories about people, not issues.
3. If you find a strong character, stick with them, even if it means scrapping everything else you had planned.

How do you get someone to open up to you on camera? How do you get them to "forget" that the camera is there?

You have to give as much as you're asking of people. You have to show that you're invested, if you're asking people to share their deepest, darkest secrets, you better be willing to share a few of your own. You get people to forget the camera is there by *always* having it with you, and always having it rolling.

What are your best three interviewing tricks?

1. Ask dumb questions. Don't try to show how smart you are—that only puts people on guard and makes them careful about what they say. Ask the simple questions that most people (i.e., your audience) are afraid to ask because they think they're already supposed to know the answer.
2. I don't know if it's a trick as much as how my mind works, but I tend to interview in a very non-linear fashion. I will ask a follow-up to my first question as, say, my sixth question . . . I keep going back to things that the interviewee thinks we've moved on from. It's very organic, in an all-over-the-place sort of way.
3. Listen. Don't think about the camera, the lighting, the shot, the background noise. Your job is to listen as much as it is to interrogate. People can tell when you're listening. If you aren't, they wonder why they're bothering to tell you anything.

When you are in the field, what is in your gear bags? What gear do you guys use at Vice news?

Varies from shoot to shoot, but most of the time it's a Canon C300, a 5D, and an XF 105; several GoPros and mounts, first aid kit, beef jerky, Emergen-C, and baby wipes.

How do you organize your material in post-production?

We rarely transcribe our material unless it's a lengthy interview. Translation on the other hand, there's tons and tons of that. We rely on having strong field notes to help our editors know what's worth digging into and what they shouldn't waste their time on.

You have produced a lot of video. What works for Web video in general?

Pieces where the audience feels some sort of connection not only with the subjects but with the makers. If it lacks a feeling of authorship, if it just feels like some sort of "product," people feel less invested in watching it.

What overall advice would you give to new video producers?

If you think that the films you've made aren't as good as they could have been, you're on the right track. Don't get too comfortable.

CHAPTER 6

Post-Production

For non-fiction video producers, storytelling often does not truly begin until the post-production stage. During reporting or pre-production, you gather facts and determine the focus of your shooting. During production, you shoot interviews and b-roll. But editing, or post-production, is when you combine, arrange, highlight, sequence, and eliminate footage to craft compelling visual stories.

When I started editing video early in my career, I used analog tape editing systems that required video stories to be put together linearly. These systems consisted of two tape decks: a source tape deck and a master tape deck. To put my stories together, I would cue up the desired raw footage in the source deck, play that clip and press record on the master tape deck. When the clip ended, I pressed stop on both decks. Then I would cue up my next clip on the source deck and, again, I would press play on the source deck and record on the master deck. This process was repeated, clip after clip, in a line until my story was complete. This became known as *linear editing*. If I made a mistake or wanted to make changes in the middle of my story, I would have to rewind my master footage and *punch in* a replacement clip. This was an extremely slow and arduous process.

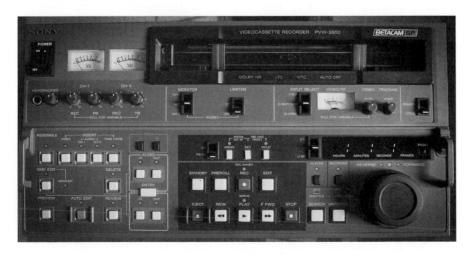

Figure 6.1
Before video editing software was developed, producers used tape decks like these to edit their stories.

Modern editing software such as Final Cut Pro, Avid, and Premiere Pro are called *non-linear* editing (NLE) systems. These digital tools allow editors to quickly add, move, and delete video clips without having to punch in footage over a master sequence. All modern editing systems provide the features needed to edit even the most ambitious projects. While I personally use Adobe Premiere Pro to edit my work, the principles discussed in this chapter are applicable to all software and editing systems. Once you have learned one software package and understand editing philosophy, it will not be difficult to move onto another system.

Technical workflow. Managing media is one of the most important, yet most commonly ignored, aspects of video editing. Computers store data in a precise and structured way, and editors must be mindful of where they place raw footage, images, audio, and project files on their hard drives or they will risk losing valuable footage or work. Understanding how media works with an NLE and how to manage raw footage and other assets are the first steps in being a successful video editor.

The following guide is a step-by-step model for organizing media for all of your video projects. If you are a freelance or independent producer, this methodology should work very well for you. However, if you are in an established media organization, you may have to follow a slightly different protocol. The important thing to remember is that you must be extremely organized and diligent about saving and archiving your projects. Otherwise, you will eventually lose important footage. Let me reiterate this point: you *will* lose footage and complete projects if you do not handle media with care.

Figure 6.2

Footage shot on any camera can be edited using almost any modern editing software package.

Step one: get at least two hard drives. Always have two copies of your raw footage and your project files stored on separate hard drives in different physical locations. This will ensure that if one copy is destroyed, you will have a backup ready for use. Hard drives fail and data can easily become corrupted. Computers get lost or stolen. Apartments and offices get flooded. There are many threats to the security and integrity of your footage. A second copy of your files gives you protection and peace of mind.

Repeat the following steps on each of your hard drives for each of your video projects, regardless of length or complexity. Complete these steps *before* you begin any editing.

1. *Create a project folder*. Name this folder with an appropriate slug or short title. For example, "Education Project." Your project folder will hold all the assets—footage, music, photos, archival footage, scripts—that you have and may use for your project.

Figure 6.3
I use several external hard drives to store and back up media.

Figure 6.4
Sample file structure of a video project.

2. *Inside the project folder, create the following folders:*

- *Video*. This folder will hold all of the footage that you shot for your video project. If you shot on multiple days, create subfolders labeled with the appropriate date. I use this naming convention to date subfolders: year-month-day. The video folder will also hold any footage that you may use in your project, such as archival footage.
- *Images*. This folder will hold any photos, graphics, logos, or illustrations that you may use in your project.
- *Audio*. This folder will hold any audio other than the audio recorded in your video clips. These files may include recorded phone calls, archival radio broadcasts, music, and other audio sources.
- *Scripts*. This folder will hold all your transcriptions and the scripts you produce for your story.
- *Exports*. This folder will hold all the exported versions of your story when you are done editing.
- *Scratch*. Some NLEs will require or ask for a scratch disc or folder. During the course of video editing, software applications will create files that are stored on your hard drive for the program to run properly. If your NLE requires a scratch folder, select this one. You can also, in some cases, use your project folder as your scratch folder.

3. Copy all your video footage into the appropriate subfolders in your *Video* folder. Copy all your photos and graphics in your *Images* folder. Copy all your music and other audio files into your *Audio* folder. Copy all your transcriptions and scripts into your *Scripts* folder. *Do not use video, images, or audio you may have stored on applications such as iPhoto or iTunes.*

Be sure to complete these steps on both of the hard drives you have designated to use for your project. Once you have completed these steps, you are ready to open up your NLE and import your footage for editing. It is important that you keep all your files in their appropriate folders. Do not move files around after you have imported them into your NLE. This will cause your media to go offline or become lost.

TRANSCRIPTIONS, SCRIPTS, AND STORYBOARDS

Transcriptions. Whether your stories are narrated or non-narrated, your interviews will provide vital information, details, emotion, and narrative elements needed to tell your story. It is absolutely necessary when producing long-form video stories to transcribe all of your interviews *verbatim*. This includes in-scene interviews and impromptu discussions that occur in your b-roll.

Scanning through interviews in your NLE is cumbersome and ineffective. A word-by-word transcription can be read, highlighted, marked up, cut up, and is searchable. Transcriptions take a considerable amount of time to complete, but do not skip this fundamental step. You will lose important quotes or become easily overwhelmed by your material without transcriptions.

Figure 6.5

Transcriptions should be verbatim and include time codes

Speaker 1:	Well, to modify a little bit, I think the photographers can do the base levels, too, if they have the opportunity to do that. If the reporter is live blogging and tweeting, shoot the clip for them kind of thing. Everybody look at each other's workload and make those assessments. Do I think that it will be everybody doing everything? I hope not because everybody should have an expertise. Because once you try to do everything well, you'll do nothing well.
	I think you need to be specialized. This is a total stupid analogy, but do you ever watch Top Chef, or not Top Chef, Chopped? They always have the people that aren't pastry chefs, and it's like you never have a great chef and a great pastry chef all in one. You have a great chef and a great pastry chef. Can the pastry chef do the savory dishes? Yeah, but they're usually not as good as the chef that does them all the time. They always end making a crumble, but they're not going to make the soufflés. Do you know what I mean?
	It's the same here. The photographers will make the soufflé and the reporters will most likely do the crumble. I don't know if you know that a crumble is much easier than making a soufflé, but that's the whole point. I think that [00:08:00] money is driving lots of things, and lack of staffing and resources will make some of that almost impossible.
Speaker 2:	You get specialization, if possible.
Speaker 1:	I do think that . . . I don't know what to say because we talked about the other night, but I know that [inaudible 0:08:20] because people like [inaudible 00:08:22] the other night and we were talking about that. What I think the trend in newsrooms is to take the digital work and bring it to the reporters, and that's making . . . this would seem the photographer is redundant.

Figure 6.5
(Continued)

What I want to see is more photographers being made to be better reporters because the good thing is we live in a digital world, which is why they're trying to make the reporters more visually savvy. To me, logically, it would be smarter to make the photographers better reporters and better writers. That's going to feel backwards. I'm totally biased. I'm a photographer. I'm guilty as charged and all of that, but if it's the digital world and you have really sophisticated visual storytellers that maybe aren't the best writers or reporters because they haven't had the training, why would you throw them away and take substandard? No, again, there are reporters here that take good pictures. I'm not saying that, but that's not their expertise.

Tips for transcriptions:

- Make sure your transcriptions are verbatim. Summarizing or writing "close enough" quotes defeats the purpose of doing a proper transcription.
- Mark your transcriptions with the time code every 1 or 2 minutes. This will help you to find your quotes quickly in your NLE.
- Include "umms" and other verbal pauses or ticks. A quote on paper may sound a lot better than it actually does in video. Marking these moments will allow you to quickly scan your transcriptions to see if your interviews are clear and usable.
- Always number the pages of your transcripts. Page numbers will help you to locate quotes more quickly later. They will also be used when you are organizing your interviews in your NLE.
- Transcribe your footage as soon as you can, preferably right after you return from your shoot. Do not wait until the end of production to begin transcriptions. By that time, the amount of footage you have shot may become too overwhelming, prompting you to cut corners and not properly transcribe your footage.

Once you have transcribed all of your interviews, you must read them thoroughly. Pick out and highlight significant quotes or sound bites to be used in your story. During the first reading of my transcripts, I am very liberal with what I highlight. I am looking for any emotional, insightful, or funny quotes; colorful anecdotes; or descriptive elements that can be used as narration in the story. I like to use a yellow highlighter to mark these quotes. Alongside the highlights, I write a word or a short phrase to summarize the quote. This way, as I refer to my transcripts, I can quickly scan for themes or ideas.

Speaker 1:	That time, the time that it takes to do the video. What I have struggled with here, I feel like I can . . . it's like the re-education every single time there's another project is that all of the field reporting needs to be done. That would be done for the story. All of the visuals times a gazillion needs to be done for the video, then all of the editing and all of the picture editing times another thousand needs to be done in order for you to have a finished product.
	It's no longer bringing a photographer in at the last week. They need to be with you from the beginning. I think there's a little bit of resistance to that. This is my story and I'm going to let you in right at the end. We'll get my amazing story and you make beautiful pictures to go with it. That happens as opposed to we're going to start from the very beginning and we're going to work this together and we're a team.
	You are now the producer on this video as opposed to just the print reporter. That transition has been difficult because then the time is due. Now, all of a sudden, not only do you have this photographer out of the mix, the reporter is out of the mix.
	We've had them [inaudible 0:13:58]. It's like, "Well, they haven't written the story yet" [00:14:00] because they spent all their time transcribing and helping write the script, or editing, or looking up people, or whatever it may be. I'm not answering your question to the degree that I think you . . .
Speaker 2:	No, no, no. Just keep on going. You were just giving reasons why it's expensive and . . .
Speaker 1:	It's the time and I think to do anything well . . . they know what it takes as you start to invest in the reporting, you need to invest that and more in the video. That is yet to be understood. We, right now, are driven by print deadlines. The story is going to run. Therefore, the video needs to run. Even though the story is only going to take a week to report and write, it will take the video 2 weeks or 3, depending on the level of video, how complicated it is visually to articulate.
	If it's like fish in a barrel, it might be 2 weeks, but if it's like you're really making some serious creative leaps to get it to be, it might take 3. We're hog tight then by that print. There are times when we say, "Nope, there's nothing wrong

Figure 6.6

Potentially usable soundbites have been highlighted in this transcription.

Figure 6.6
(Continued)

> with the print." Then there's a little bit of mark but it has to run the print. It's like, "Well, it doesn't really have to run with the print." Particularly if it is Sunday, our biggest traffic day is Monday morning but, yet, we'll put our biggest stuff in the paper on Sunday, which is our biggest readership, but we'll put the Web thing with it as well. By Monday morning, they've got a new Lion's coach and that thing is gone from the Web site so you'll never even see the thing that you just spent 3 weeks on. It's ridiculous.

After you have read your transcriptions, you must select the quotes to use in your final story. The first read of your transcriptions will yield many potential quotes, but a second pass must be more refined and focused. As you read your transcriptions, you may find that your sources repeat information throughout the interview. They may articulate a thought more clearly the second or third time they answer your question. You must highlight the best of these quotes to use. What is the most clear, powerful, descriptive, and articulate quote? I will mark these in my transcript with a star, or for longer projects, I will write them on a sticky note. These will be the quotes that get selected and *subclipped* in my NLE.

Figure 6.7
Important themes or points are marked on the transcription and on note cards.

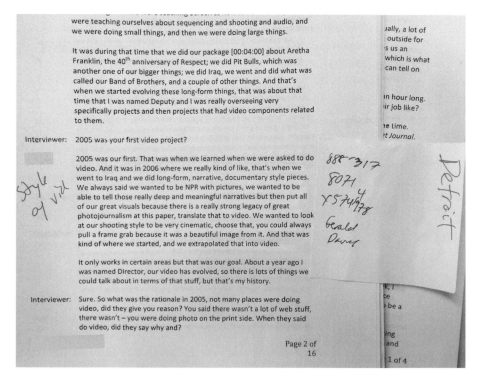

Subclipping. Subclipping is the process in video editing that separates your usable material from the rest of the raw footage. For example, you may shoot 10 hours of raw footage for an 8-minute film. From these 10 hours, you may only want to subclip or select 1 hour of potentially usable footage. This process helps to manage the mountain of material that producers invariable shoot in the field. Subclipping is akin to highlighting notes or other documents for a print story.

Every editor has their own way of dealing with soundbites and subclipping. My process is related directly to the note taking I have done in my transcriptions. Once I have highlighted my key soundbites in my transcriptions, I find and subclip them in my NLE. From an hour-long interview, I may only select 5 to 6 minutes of usable quotes.

Keeping subclips organized is important, as you may make hundreds for a single video story. I name my subclips with this convention: "INT—Name— Transcription Page Number—Note." For example, a subclip may be called "INT Johnson P12 Fundraising." Here, I know that "INT" means that this clip is an interview. This is an important note, as you will be subclipping b-roll or action featuring your characters as well. "Johnson" is the name of my source. "P12" is page 12 of his interview where I originally highlighted this quote. It is important to mark the page number from the interview in case you want to refer to his full answer later. "Fundraising" means that he is talking about fundraising for his political campaign. These notes can be used as an effective organizing tool in your NLE. You can search for the keyword "fundraising" to quickly retrieve all quotes about fundraising from all of your interviews.

After subclipping your interviews, you must organize these clips into bins or folders in your NLE. For interviews, I prefer to organize my folders by interviewee's last name. I will create a folder for each source I have interviewed. In these folders, I may create subfolders to divide my interview subclips into themes or categories. As you go through the process of subclipping and organizing your clips into folders, you will find that your footage becomes much more manageable. Rather than scrubbing through hours of interviews, you now have an organized, searchable collection of potentially usable soundbites.

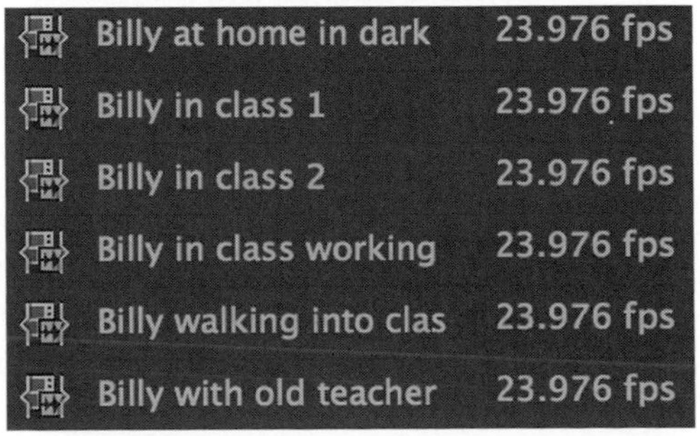

Billy at home in dark	23.976 fps	
Billy in class 1	23.976 fps	
Billy in class 2	23.976 fps	
Billy in class working	23.976 fps	
Billy walking into clas	23.976 fps	
Billy with old teacher	23.976 fps	

Figure 6.8

Larger clips should be logged into smaller subclips.

Figure 6.9

An organized bin of subclipped footage.

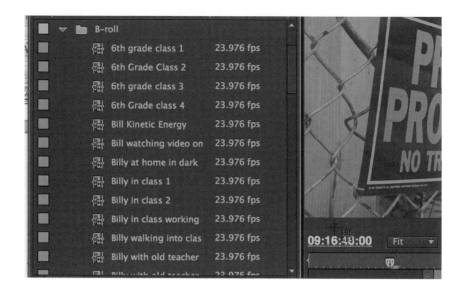

Scripts. A script is a detailed roadmap for video editors. Even if you are editing your own work, you will need to write a script before editing your story. Often called a "paper edit," scripts allow you to arrange your selected soundbites into a sequence that makes logical sense. Scripts also allow you to quickly read your story to ensure that you have presented all relevant information. Scripts should include exact transcriptions of the soundbites you will use. If your story is narrated, scripts should include exact narration as well.

Write your scripts in a program such as Word or Google Docs. This will allow you to edit your ideas and your sequence of quotes quickly. Editing a script in Word is much faster than editing footage in an NLE. Some editors prefer to work directly on their NLE timeline, but I find that working without a paper script ultimately is more time consuming and presents too many opportunities for losing the focus of my story.

Figure 6.10

The script for the Video Now *video.*

Video Now: Purpose and Methodology

When the *Chicago Sun-Times* cut its entire photo staff in May 2013, owners said the layoffs were part of a plan to increase video production. The *Sun-Times* was making video a big editorial and sales focus, no longer just an afterthought.

The paper's move, while unpopular with photographers, was not completely surprising. Online video is huge, and it has the potential to make a lot of money, at least in theory.

However, the *Sun-Times* did not say what kinds of videos they would produce, who would produce them, and what kind of return on investment they hoped to make.

Like Chicago, the *New York Times*, the *Wall Street Journal*, and other papers have also been building up their video teams. Startups like Now This News are banking on video to reverse the industry's downward slide.

Newspapers agree that video is important, but there seems to be no consensus on how to roll it out. Organizations large, small, and startup are figuring out how to produce news videos, and how to make them profitable. TV news has been around for decades, but online video is still young.

With that in mind, the Tow Center set out to produce this report, *Video Now*, to find out what was really happening in newsrooms. For months, we travelled across the country. We watched journalists make video. We spoke to editors about their goals and challenges. And we whittled down hundreds of hours of footage into the stories on this site.

A few things about this report:

First, it is not exhaustive, nor complete. There are . . .

Radio edit. Once you have written your script and are satisfied that your story is complete and compelling, you can begin to edit your interviews in your timeline. Typically, I edit all of my interviews into my timeline before I deal with b-roll or action. This sequence of soundbites is often referred to as a *radio edit* because, at this point, you are primarily dealing with the audio of your interviews. Using your script as a guideline, choose the corresponding interview clips from your bins of subclips. Trim the audio to remove any unwanted soundbites and place these trimmed quotes into your timeline.

Radio edits provide you with the first version of your story. As you lay your soundbites into the timeline, listen to how they sound together. Are your soundbites powerful and effective? Do they finish in strong, complete sentences? Or do they trail off at the end? Often, a transcription will fail to capture the nuances of the spoken word. A radio edit may not sound as sharp, precise, or impactful as you had imagined in your script. If this is the case, you may want to pick alternate soundbites or rewrite your script.

It is important to get your radio edit to the point where your story is clear and comprehensible, even without b-roll. A good radio edit will only become a better story with action placed on top of it. A radio edit that is flat or does not

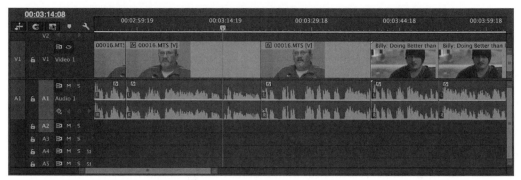

Figure 6.11
Interviews are laid down first into a "radio edit" version of the story.

make sense will not likely be salvageable with b-roll. When I have completed my radio edit, I will adjust the audio levels of my soundbites so that they are nearly equal to each other (peaking at around –12db in the timeline). Inconsistent audio levels will distract listeners, and may give more weight or prominence to sources with louder soundbites.

Managing B-roll. B-roll, or action footage, must be organized as carefully as interview footage. Rather than working from a transcript, editors must watch all their footage to make selects of potentially usable scenes. It is important not to review your footage too quickly because you may miss important moments or usable shots. The more focused and diligent you were about shooting footage, the less work you will have in post-production. Some video producers have a "tape is cheap" mentality and will overshoot in the field. This will prove to be costlier as you must spend much more time reviewing footage in post-production.

All editors manage b-roll with their own methods and strategies. But, as with interview footage, you must create a sensible system of organization. Hours of b-roll will become too overwhelming to manage if you do not organize your footage early on. You must subclip and label your b-roll as you did with interview clips. You may shoot hours and hours of great action, but you may only have a few minutes in your final piece. Being organized will allow you to quickly edit the most powerful and relevant footage.

I generally label my b-roll with this convention: "Character—Action—Type of shot." For example: "Johnson—writing speech—WS." These three notes will help me to quickly search for my characters, find active scenes, and identify the type of shot I can use to edit my scenes. My next clip may be "Johnson—hands writing speech—CU." By quickly scanning my subclips labels, I can see that I have both a wide shot of the speech writing and a detailed shot of my character's hands. Once

Figure 6.12
An organized bin of b-roll footage.

I have subclipped my b-roll, I organize the clips into folders based on scenes such as "script writing," "first TV debate," "shaking hands with voters," and so on.

Tips for organizing b-roll:

- *Do not try to be too precise when subclipping.* You do not want to accidentally cut off a process or action in mid-motion. Shots will be trimmed later in the timeline.
- *Be sure to make discreet subclips of wide shots, medium shots, close ups, reaction shots, and POV shots.* Try not to grab a single 20-minute clip of raw footage and label it "speech at rally." You will still have to watch this clip over and over to get the shots you will need to edit your scene.
- *Look for establishing shots, cutaways, and general transition shots.* Wide shots of locations make for great transitions from scene to scene. Reaction shots are invaluable for covering edits. Make a folder of these to be used throughout your piece.
- *Make notes about the footage you still need.* It is common, if time and budget permit, to get pick-up shots, or additional b-roll that you missed earlier on. Do you need more establishing shots? Do you need more transitions? Do you need one more scene? Make a note and be sure to get these shots.

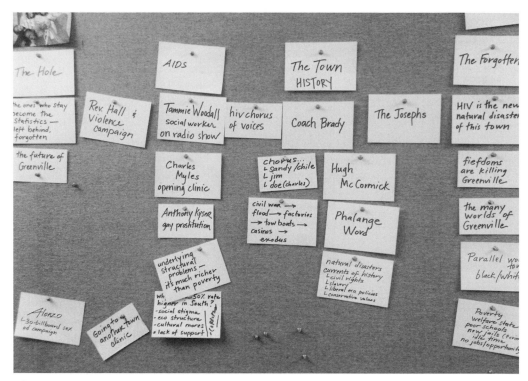

Figure 6.13
Storyboards are a powerful tool for organizing a narrative.

Storyboarding. A script is a powerful tool for organizing your story, but for more complicated or longer films, you will need to use a storyboard to arrange your ideas, characters, acts, and arcs. A storyboard is a visual tool for organizing scenes and the narrative flow of your story. Storyboards work best when they are large, colorful, and tactile.

I prefer to use colored notecards or sticky notes to represent each scene in my story. As I narrow down the scenes that are relevant to my story, I can easily move these scenes around or delete them altogether. This process is much faster than editing and moving scenes in an NLE.

Storyboards give you a bird's eye view of the story, making it easier to see the flow of the narrative. The use of notecards allows for quick and easy rearranging of your storyline. When we were editing *deepsouth*, we went through many iterations of our story before we began editing in our NLE. Avoid using computer-based or online storyboarding applications. These are great for sharing ideas remotely with other producers. However, I have found nothing easier or more efficient than using an offline storyboard with notecards to organize my work.

Figure 6.14
The final storyboard used for deepsouth.

Editing style. Over time and with practice, you will develop your own unique editing style. Video editors, just like writers, eventually develop specific techniques and forms that give their films a distinctive voice. Some editors are known for frenetic, energetic cutting. Others are known for their thoughtful pacing. But before you can develop your own style, you must first become a fundamentally-sound video editor. You must learn and become proficient in the following areas:

- *Technology.* You must become comfortable using your preferred video editing software or the system used at your news organization. You must know the various tools and features well enough to edit without thinking about the software. You must understand file management and how computers, hard drives, and video work together.
- *Project organization.* You must be diligent about organizing your projects—transcribing footage, subclipping interviews and b-roll, and organizing your clips into folders.
- *Best practices.* Just as there are grammatical rules for writing, there are also best practices and procedures for editing video. Good video editing serves the story and the viewer, and produces a film that is easy to understand, organized, and devoid of technical errors.

BEST PRACTICES

Cutting down. After organizing your interviews and b-roll into bins of subclips, you can begin to edit your video. As previously discussed, the first part of editing is to lay down the radio edit of your story. If your soundbites make sense in your timeline, then you can begin to add b-roll and develop scenes.

I often use the analogy of rock sculpture to describe video editing. Like a sculptor, video editors start with a massive amount of unformed material. But by chiseling away at the footage, eliminating some material while refining other elements, the editor eventually produces a refined and complete work. Editors produce various versions of the video story during the editing process: assembly, rough cut, fine cut, and final cut. Each version removes material from and refines the previous version. The first edit or cut of your story will never be your final version.

- *Assembly edit.* The assembly edit is a broad and liberal edit of your film. Unrefined b-roll and scenes are brought down into the timeline to go along with your interviews or narration. This version is used to determine which scenes work, which action makes sense, and whether you have enough b-roll to illustrate your story. Assembly edits can be many times longer than the final version of the story, and the editing can be choppy and unrefined.
- *Rough cut.* The term *rough cut* can be misleading. A rough cut is a version that has had most of the extraneous scenes and footage edited or removed from the assembly. Rough cuts are only "rough" in the sense that they have not been polished with final credits, mixing, or color correction. They are well-edited and do not possess many technical errors or missing elements. Rough cuts present producers and editors an opportunity to view a more complete version of their story to make further edits, script changes, and other refinements.

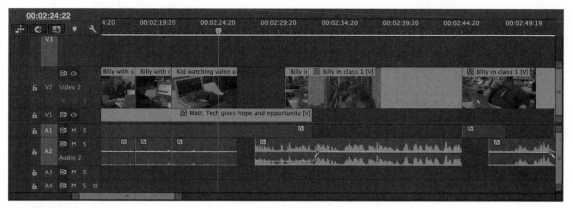

Figure 6.15
An example of an assembly edit.

- *Fine cut.* The fine cut is, for all intents and purposes, the final version of the film. This version is a final opportunity for producers to make sure that they have smoothed out any technical errors, clarified any confusing scenes from the rough cut, and made sure that the audio has been properly mixed. The fine cut is often only missing some final color correction and the beginning titles and closing credits.
- *Final cut.* As the name denotes, the final cut is the finished version of your film that is ready for airing or distribution online. The final cut is referred as being "locked." At this stage, the video story is clear and complete, the audio is well-mixed, and the footage has been carefully edited and color-corrected.

Editing rules and tips. As you progress from the assembly to the final cut stages of your story, keep the following rules or best practices in mind. Regardless of your personal style, the pacing of your story, or the look-and-feel of your film, these guidelines and editing tips will help you produce professional-quality videos with high production value.

- *Mix up wide shots and close ups.* In a previous chapter, we discussed the importance of getting a variety of shots: wide shots, medium shots, and close ups. You must use these shots thoughtfully in your editing. When putting clips together to form a scene, edit from a close up to a wide shot, a wide shot to a close up, or a close up to a close up. Avoid editing from a wide shot to a wide shot.

   Wide shots can give the viewer great context, but it is important to follow a wide shot with a detail shot. Think about how your eyes naturally scan any environment. When you step into a room, you will first take a wide look at the entire room. Then, you will immediately

Figure 6.16
An example of a final cut.

scan for a specific object or person. If you try, you will find that it is hard to avoid focusing on details in the room. As an editor, you must cut to close ups to satisfy the viewers' need for details and close ups.

- *Lead with audio.* When you cut from one scene to the next, or transition between scenes, lead with audio. In Figure 6.18 notice that the audio from the b-roll plays before the viewer sees the video from the b-roll. This technique is called a "J-Cut." An "L-Cut" is when the audio from your video clip continues to play after the video has been cut. Leading with audio makes for smoother transitions than straight cuts.
- *Cut on completed action.* Avoid cutting in the middle of an uncompleted action, as it can be jarring for the viewer. If your character is reaching for a cup of coffee, let the viewer see the completed action before you cut away. Unrefined edits like these disrupt the story and pull the viewer out of the scene. Wait until your character has grabbed the cup of coffee before cutting away. This does not mean that you can only edit on

Figure 6.17
Edit from wide shots to close ups to provide context and detail in your scene.

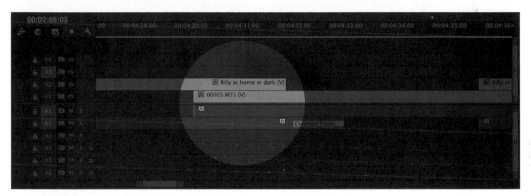

Figure 6.18
An example of an L-cut.

stationary shots; this will make your videos dull. You can and should edit on motion, but be sure that the motion is complete.

- *Dissolves have meaning.* New editors tend to overuse cross dissolves to transition between two clips. Dissolves should be used carefully and appropriately. A dissolve is the equivalent of an ellipsis in writing—it connotes a passing of time in the action. Often, you will see cooking videos dissolving between shots of the chef stirring or mixing ingredients. These cross-dissolves signify that some time has passed for the chef to make his dish. Avoid using dissolves without their intended meaning.

- *Let the story breathe.* Videos should be a carefully paced series of interviews and narration mixed together with active scenes. Avoid putting soundbites too close together. Your video should breathe—there should be space between thoughts and scenes, and you should have moments of b-roll without any narration. Putting interviews and narration next to each other throughout your film will exhaust and overwhelm the viewer.

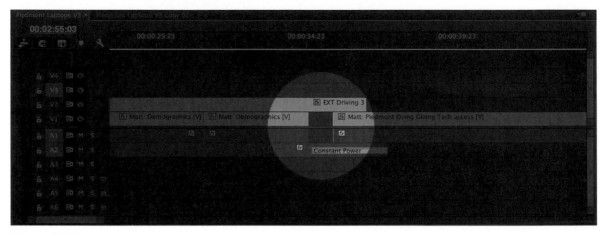

Figure 6.19
Put spaces between your soundbites to create a natural rhythm to your interviews.

■ *Use minimal text.* Viewers watch videos to see action, not to read words. Do not rely on text to advance your story or provide too much context. Text should be used to identify your sources and to give minimal contextual information such as the location and date of your story. In longer-form documentaries, text can be used to provide some deeper background information. But, as a rule, avoid using text in place of interviews or b-roll. Your viewers will grow tired of having the action of your video interrupted.

■ *Mix audio well.* Audio is, by far, the most important technical element of your video story. Poorly recorded and edited audio will not be tolerated by your viewers. When putting together your radio edits, make sure that all your interviews are mixed to peak at around –12db. Avoid having certain interviews louder than others. This will frustrate your viewers, and, editorially, it may serve to give more weight or value to your louder sources. Also, avoid having b-roll, music, or other audio conflict with your interviews or narration.

■ *Color correct footage.* While all effort must be made to properly expose and white balance your footage in the field, you will always shoot some imperfect video. In post-production, be sure to correct these exposure and white balance problems. Footage that is too dark or the wrong tint will be distracting to the viewer.

Figure 6.20
The image on the left is straight from the camera. The image on the right has been corrected to achieve better exposure and white balance.

SOCIAL MEDIA

Whether producing independently or as a part of a larger news organization, journalists are increasingly being required to promote their stories online and on social media. Promotion of your video, especially if it is a long-form documentary film, should begin as soon as you start production. It is too late to build an audience after you have exported your final cut, and it is short-sighted to only rely on your current fans or viewership.

"We aggressively look for places where people are. That's a big shift in a short amount of time," says Pam Johnston, Director of Audience Development for *Frontline*.

> It wasn't very long ago where it was like, we're on television and we're on our Web site, and if you would like to find us, that is where you can come visit us. I think that there's been a shift, which is: if you want them, you better go get them. Not only do we spend lots of time and attention cultivating our social media audiences on Twitter and on Facebook and on Instagram, but we're always developing new communities. Is Pinterest right for *Frontline*? There's a lot of people there, a lot of women there. Does it make makes sense for us? We need to be really smart about where we spend our limited time and limited resources.

Documentary films can take months or years to report, shoot, and edit. Social media can help journalists to report their stories, develop an audience for their films, and remain active and relevant, even if they are not producing daily news stories. During the production of *deepsouth*, Lisa Biagiotti and

Figure 6.21

We used social media platforms such as Facebook and Twitter to promote deepsouth *before the film was completed.*

I were dedicated to building a strong social media presence well before the release. By the time *deepsouth* was completed, we already had built an avid following and an audience hungry to see the documentary. With no marketing budget, we sold out our world premiere screening in Washington, DC. Our social network has brought the film to dozens of cities throughout the United States, the UK, and South America.

Special features first. When DVDs first became popular, they were often packaged with features such behind-the-scenes films and bonus material from the movie. Today, an effective and important strategy for building an audience is to release this "extra" material in advance of the film's completion. This material can be shareable, discussed, and promoted by your followers online. More importantly, it can help to build momentum for your film.

For *deepsouth*, we used the Jux.com blogging platform to release material from our film. Jux allowed us to post updates from the road, raw video teaser clips, trailers, and research that we had compiled. Additionally, as interest for the film grew, we used the site to reach out for more sources and data. The site worked two ways: it brought the film to a growing audience, and it brought sources and communities to us. Our site was integral to building a grassroots marketing campaign that resulted in filling most of our screening events.

FUNDRAISING

While you are finishing one project, you should already be planning and raising funds for your next one. As newsrooms shrink and resources become limited, more video projects are being funded by non-traditional sources: grants, sponsorships, and crowd-funding. Even large publications such as NPR and *The Seattle Times* have turned to foundations and online campaigns to raise money for important journalism projects. Increasingly, journalists will have to acquire most of the capital required for their films, rather than assuming that a news organization will fund their project.

In 2013, I founded Columbia Visuals (www.columbiavisuals.com), a blog that covers best practices for photo and video journalism. Our story topics include the creative, technical, legal, and funding challenges facing video producers. This blog is a free resource and updated weekly. There are several links to grants and awards for filmmakers on the site. The post from Columbia Visuals below is about Kickstarter, one of the most popular crowd-funding platforms today.

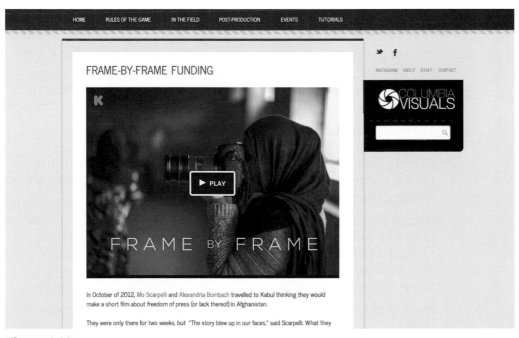

Figure 6.22

Columbia Visuals (www.columbiavisuals.com) is a free online resource for visual journalists.

"Frame-by-Frame Funding" by Jika Gonzalez, Columbia Visuals Staff Writer

In October of 2012, Mo Scarpelli and Alexandria Bombach travelled to Kabul thinking they would make a short film about freedom of press (or lack thereof) in Afghanistan.

They were only there for two weeks, but "The story blew up in our faces," said Scarpelli. What they saw was an emerging free press in the war-torn country, and a handful of Afghan journalists behind it.

Most of these reporters and photographers are people that trained themselves and learned from the international press corps, explained Scarpelli, but as the troops pull out, so does the international media, and it is up to local journalists to keep coverage of Afghanistan in the press.

Now Scarpelli and Bombach are going back to film *Frame by Frame*, a feature-length documentary backed by a successful Kickstarter campaign, about the recent revolution in Afghan photojournalism. The film will focus on four photojournalists, each from a different background.

Before trying Kickstarter, the filmmakers looked for sponsorships and applied for grants, without much success. Bombach sold her car, and dipped into her savings to get the money for the trip to film the trailer, which cost between $12,000 and $15,000.

"It was simply too much money to fund it ourselves," says Scarpelli. "The fixer fees alone were too expensive."

Their Kickstarter campaign asked for $40,000, but they received $70,301. Had they not gotten the extra thirty thousand dollars, they would have had to hold another fundraiser after they got back. Instead, now they're in "full production mode."

The initial asking amount, the first $40,000, will pay for travel, five weeks in Kabul, equipment, translators, and fixers. The extra funds are allowing them to seek legal counsel during production, instead of after the film is done. Looking down the road, it should also be enough for an assistant editor and a sound engineer.

On their return trip to Kabul, they will also take new shooting gear, which is likely to include two Canon 5-D Mark III and accessories, as well as more powerful editing equipment (right now they both work on laptops). Though the trailer was shot on Canon C300s, the filmmakers decided to go for the DSLRs, which they are more comfortable using and less expensive.

Scarpelli gave us five tips she says are key when fundraising for your project:

- *Find the nut graf of your project.* It's a good exercise in thinking about why you're doing this to begin with, explains Scarpelli. When you want to justify the fundraising, you have to come up with the nut graf of the story you want to tell. "I really believe in the story," says Scarpelli. "I still get shivers when I think about it."

- *Pitch everywhere.* Send your Kickstarter campaign to blogs and online publications that have an audience for your story. "Pitch all day, every day," she says.
- *Stick with it.* You have to be persistent, and you have to consistently "push people" before, during, and after the campaign. Scarpelli made it her full time job to reach out to everyone she knew about their project and Kickstarter campaign.
- *Seek media partners.* They reached out to specific sites like MediaStorm and Upworthy, and requested support for the campaign by asking their audiences and communities to fund their film. You need people to vouch for you. As an example, Brian Storm, the founder and executive producer of MediaStorm, "was very supportive," explained Scarpelli. There was also a huge push from Upworthy at the very end of the campaign. "By noon the day before it ended, our emails blew up," says Scarpelli.
- *Get rid of self-doubt.* When you're on a long term project there tends to be moments of self-doubt, but if you're asking people for money to fund your work, you have to be convinced that it's worth it. You can't be insecure when you ask people for money. "Ask yourself: Why should anyone care?" says Scarpelli. If you're going to ask for money, you need to "mean business, and you have to love the idea behind your story."

Q&A with the Experts: Joe Lindquist, Editor of *deepsouth*

Figure 6.23
Joe Lindquist, Editor of deepsouth.

In a documentary film, what is the role of the editor?
The role of the film editor in a documentary is to contextualize; you need to make sense of the hours of footage that has just been placed in your hands. In the documentary world, there can be many hours of footage, so it's no small task. Narratively speaking, I often think that the last draft of a script is written in the editing room. But when it comes to documentary, it's often the first.

You might be working off of an outline, or you may have been given a loose sense of structure, but the process always begins the same way. It's just you and the footage. It's up to you to identify what is most compelling about what you're watching, and it's up to you to streamline and package it into a compelling story. In that way, the role of an editor, on any platform and in any medium, is always the same: marry your sound and images in a sequence that makes sense to another human being. Or at least, it holds their attention for an hour and a half.

What are some mistakes that shooters make that make your job harder?
Having an abundance of footage, or coverage, can be a blessing and a curse for me. It's a blessing in that you have so many options, and a curse in that you have way *too many* options. I think the appearance of plentiful coverage may not be as useful as it seems. Sometimes the shooter will try to overcompensate, and give you as many shot choices as possible, which shows up in the footage in negative ways.

All too often, I see raw footage that simply doesn't stay put, shots that don't hold for very long, and a camera that seems to be constantly jumping and trying not to miss any of the action. You end up not getting very much of the action at all. Like an editor who has so many choices, the shooter has even more. You need to make decisions on who you're covering and simply stick to it. Relax. Listen. And let your subject draw you in.

What kind of footage should shooters remember to get to make edits easier or more compelling?
The shooter's attention should be drawn to the main point of action. Whatever lays before you—an interview, a conversation among multiple subjects, or covering tons of physical action—focus on why and what you're shooting in the first place. What motivated you to be there that day? Always be adaptable because the focus can shift, but always slow your pace and listen attentively.

Before moving out of a space, especially one that you may not have access to later, try your best to get coverage of your surroundings. Establishing shots and clean ambient audio (room tone) are quite helpful.

Be sure to shoot non-speaking faces. If you are filming a conversation, it's a good idea to ask your subjects to simply continue talking to each other and purposefully film the person who is listening. Faces that aren't talking are actually quite valuable in the editing room, so get as many as you can!

How do you organize hundreds of hours of footage to prep for editing?
The first step is to back up all raw on a new drive so I always have footage in two locations. That's the golden rule.

The raw footage is usually logged by date, and I like to give it a title or heading. If I need to convert files, which I do often, I like making sure they match the raw names. Within my editing program, I create many folders and bins. I make sure I have a folder that links to all my footage (staying consistent with names). I create two kinds of sequences: a "selects" sequence and an "assembly" sequence.

"Selects" are simply clean audio or visual that can be useful to me later in the editing process. The "assembly" is a long-form scene built from my "selects." This may be comprised of many scenes as it is a first attempt at making sense of the day's footage. Keeping the assemblies and selects sequences together is a good idea for easy reference in the future. I also create separate bins for all music files and sound effects.

Every day I log in, I create new project files with a new date. Every night I log out, I save a copy of the project file on a separate drive (other than the drive the project lives on). Your editing system will probably have an auto-save feature. Make sure it's set to save files off of your main drive. If your drive should crash, you now have an adequate back up.

Do you work from a script or some kind of outline? What is your post-production workflow from the time the shooter/producer hands you footage?
As I mentioned previously, I believe the first draft of your "script" is in the edit room. Outlines are very helpful and can usually be put together with the aide of your director and producer. But nothing is better than the process of watching the footage for yourself. Unlike the director, you have the benefit of a pure, objective viewpoint, so utilize it! What am I watching? What is most compelling to me?

After you've made your own assessments, guided by the director, you can begin to revise an outline and begin to get a sense of what the narrative actually is. You won't fully know every plot turn until your assemblies begin to come together. But that's fine. You don't have to just yet.

I also use note cards, a whole lot of tacks, and big board to help organize the ever-evolving narrative as it develops. Each card usually represents a scene. Scenes change frequently, so it's nice to be able to organize the "big board" as well as your footage.

What three tips would you give to any documentary filmmaker?
Stay planted when shooting. I mentioned this earlier, but it's a very important point. Does it mean hold a shot and never move? Of course not. It means make sure your camera movements are motivated and as deliberate as possible. Erratic camera movements and shots that barely hold for a few seconds are typically on the cutting room floor. Don't be afraid to hold your shot and film your subject for minutes on end.

Love your subjects for who they are. Don't shoot "around" them. Shoot *them*! If you have the chance to get to know them off camera, make it happen. People behave differently when the cameras roll but are more at ease around people they know. So get to know them. Make friends. It may sound vague or cheesy but you can film trust. It shows up on film! Developing trust helps your footage become more organic and less stilted or contrived. Your subjects are your collaborators, so communicate! Getting to know them off camera can open up many new doors and many new ideas in the future of your movie.

What are the biggest challenges of being a video editor?

Editing documentaries is a marathon process so I try not to burn myself out too quickly. I try not to "over-watch" my sequences. I try not to over-think and get lost in options as opposed to just cutting footage. It's easy to get lost, so I make sure I have my tools and my people (producers, director) not too far away.

Communication is key, and editing, even though it is often solitary, is all about communication. It's about how the footage speaks to *you* and how you can *translate* that footage so it speaks to others. So get others involved! Screen your rough cuts.

You may not always know where your story is headed, which can be frustrating. But it can also be exciting! So always be open and let that energy motivate your choices. No matter how big or small, tell the story you set out to tell.

Feature and Narrative Storytelling

CHAPTER 7

Producing a Feature Video Story

I often joke to my graduate students that what I teach them about story-telling they already know and probably have known since early child-hood. Good narrative stories—from childhood fables to documentaries to Hollywood blockbusters—all possess the same components: a protago-nist or main character, a conflict, and a resolution. Stories are only differ-ent in style and content. Fairy tales are fiction and contain a moral message. Journalism is non-fiction and contain facts and a central idea (newspaper reporters call this idea a *nut graf*). But, structurally, good stories all follow a very similar form.

NOT THE INVERTED PYRAMID

Short, breaking news stories in newspapers and on local TV do not follow the protagonist-conflict-resolution form of storytelling. Rather, they utilize the

INVERTED PYRAMID

Most newsworthy information
Who? What? When? Where? Why? How?

Important details

Background
information

Figure 7.1

inverted pyramid structure of news writing. Journalists have used this mode of storytelling for over a century to relay news quickly. In the top part of the inverted pyramid are the most relevant, interesting, and newsworthy facts and quotes. The second part of the pyramid contains supporting details. The bottom part of the pyramid presents background information.

With the inverted pyramid, the information presented becomes less important or vital to the reader towards the end of the article or video package. This model works very well for breaking news stories, especially online where most articles are not longer than a few hundred words. For news or alerts, readers want the most important information immediately, right at the top of the story. Readers do not have to read all the way to the end to get the most important information.

For journalists who have primarily written news stories or produced news video using the inverted pyramid, transitioning to feature or narrative storytelling can be difficult. Unlike an inverted pyramid story, the most important parts of a feature or narrative are rarely at the beginning of the story. Feature videos and narrative documentaries reveal information throughout the story and build up to a climax or resolution. When watching a feature video story, viewers *must* stay to the end of the story to get *all* the pertinent information. This presents a major challenge to video storytellers, especially online where viewers have many options and distractions. How can video storytellers hold their viewers' attention when Facebook, Twitter, Netflix, and video games are just a click away?

GOOD STORIES TOLD WELL

I visited newsrooms across the United States to conduct research for the *Video Now* report, a study on the current state of video journalism. At every news organization, I asked my sources the same question: What is a good video story? Invariably, the answers I got were all some version of *a good story told well.*

Finding a good story requires thorough reporting, creative thinking, and dedication and passion on the part of the journalist. But what does it take for one to tell a story well? Video journalists must structure and present their stories in a way that gets the viewer to watch from the beginning to the very end. Understanding the protagonist-conflict-resolution structure will help you to produce stories that your viewers will want to watch in their entirety.

Figure 7.2
Newspaper photographers are increasingly tasked with producing compelling video content as well as photos.

At some point in your early childhood, you may have been told a version of this story:

> Once upon a time, there was a princess. The princess was trapped in a castle by an evil witch. But, in this land, there was a brave knight. The knight loved the princess and wanted to rescue her from the witch.
>
> One day, the knight set off for the witch's castle to save the princess. But the witch sent a fiery dragon to kill the knight. The dragon attacked the knight, but the brave knight used his sword to slay the dragon.
>
> When the knight reached the castle, he chained up the witch and freed the princess. The princess and the knight got married and they lived happily ever after.

This fairy tale, while simple, contains all the elements of a feature story: a protagonist, a conflict, and a resolution. In this story, the knight is the protagonist. The protagonist of a story has a goal, and, in this case, the knight's goal was to rescue the princess. The conflict of this story is the knight's battle with the witch and the dragon. The resolution is that the knight saves the princess and they live happily ever after. In this fairy tale, the reader must go to the very end to find out whether the knight has been successful in his quest.

If this fairy tale were written using the inverted pyramid method, it might read something like this:

> Today, a brave knight rescued a princess from the castle of the wicked witch. During the rescue operation, the knight also killed a dragon

owned by the witch. The knight was able to imprison the witch, and the princess was unharmed during the raid on the castle. The knight and princess now plan to get married.

This version of the story has all the same factual elements as the first version of the fairy tale, but it lacks tension, suspense, and drama. After the first sentence, the reader does not have to read further to know the ending. Feature and narrative stories present important information, but in a way that teases the viewer to stay until the end for the resolution or *reveal*.

You will meet many characters during your reporting. Not all of your characters can be the protagonists of your stories. Some sources will have interesting backgrounds and goals, but you must select the best sources to tell your stories. Most sources will be secondary and tertiary characters, and they will play important roles in your story. But, for your feature story to be well told and interesting to your viewers, you must clearly identify the protagonist, the protagonist's goal or quest, and the resolution to the story.

Exercise

Pick your 10 favorite books or films. These stories can be fiction or non-fiction. Identify the main character or protagonist in each story. What was the conflict? What was the resolution of the story? Did all of these stories have a clear protagonist, conflict, and resolution?

Big question. Producing feature stories can be complicated and overwhelming. Topics such as health, science, politics, and the economy are vast, confusing, and can be difficult for video storytellers to condense into a clear and focused story. Inexperienced reporters can easily get caught up in topics and ideas, and often fail to drill down to specific stories within those topics.

Figure 7.3

Kathie from deepsouth *works on a speech to be given during an important HIV/AIDS conference.*

Distilling a story from a topic requires focusing on a very specific aspect of that topic. It is difficult to produce a story about heath care, the economy, or conflict in the Middle East. These concepts are too broad. It is much easier to produce a story about the cost of Obamacare on local businesses, or what a family with unemployed parents is doing to put food on the table, or how social media aided revolutionary movements in Middle Eastern countries.

One way to organize and focus your reporting and storytelling is by answering *one big question* in your project. There are many questions to be asked and answered on any topic, but what *specific* question are you trying to answer with your story? What facts will you focus on? What will you ask your sources? What action will you demonstrate in your videos?

CASE STUDY: CAMP SUNDOWN: KIDS WITH XERODERMA PIGMENTOSUM

Craryville, NY, a rural town about 2 hours north of New York City, is home to Sundown, a camp run by Caren and Dan Mahar. At first, this sleep-away retreat seems indistinguishable from any other summer camp you might find anywhere else. Kids go swimming here, they play baseball, some stay up and tell ghost stories, and others perform in impromptu talent shows.

What makes Camp Sundown unusual is that all the campers suffer from rare genetic disorders such as Xeroderma Pigmentosum, or XP. XP is, literally, a one in a million disease that makes those afflicted deathly allergic to the sun and other UV rays. Even the slightest exposure to UV light can cause skin to

Figure 7.4
Camp Sundown in Craryville, NY.

burn and blister instantly. There is no current cure or treatment for XP, and most sufferers do not survive beyond their 20s.

I found, reported, and produced this story over the course of two summers. It was an emotionally draining and editorially challenging project. I wanted to tell the story of these kids and their families, but I wanted to make sure that I did it in an honest and sensitive way. The story would have been too easy to sensationalize, and I wanted to avoid objectifying the children. Over the course of project, I was able to interview, shoot footage, and edit a story I believe to be compelling, emotional, informative, and honest. This is how "Camp Sundown" was produced.

Finding the story. Most stories come about through solid beat reporting— sources will lead you to newsworthy events and noteworthy issues in their communities. But, occasionally, story ideas come out of general curiosity. The idea for "Camp Sundown" came to me from, of all places, a Nicole Kidman film. *The Others*, released in 2001, is a psychological thriller about ghosts and the supernatural. Nicole Kidman's character in the film has two children who are allergic to the sun and their lives are painstakingly structured to protect them from experiencing any daylight.

The Others was not a very memorable film for me, but the concept of sun allergies stuck with me long after I watched it. I had not heard of anyone being allergic to UV light before, and I assumed that the disease was fictional. I Googled some variation of the terms "sun allergies" and "allergic to light" and found some references to XP and other skin diseases such as porphyria. There were very few news stories about these diseases. I was hooked on this topic.

Reporting. My Google searches about XP gave me links to Web sites that led to message boards that eventually led me to an online brochure for Camp Sundown and the XP Society, the non-profit that Caren and Dan Mahar founded when their daughter was diagnosed with the disease. Through online research, I had learned much about the symptoms of XP, the theorized causes, and the rareness of the disease. However, I had not spoken to a single human source on the topic.

When reporting any story, *Internet searches should just be the beginning.* The Web has become a great source for information, but to find new stories you must speak to real human sources. Information and stories online have already been reported and written by someone else. Online search results should only be used for background information; they should not be considered primary sources. Had I stopped at just Googling "XP," I would not have been able to produce a video about Camp Sundown.

Gaining access. There were many challenges to gaining access to the characters in this story. Having children participate in any story is difficult because

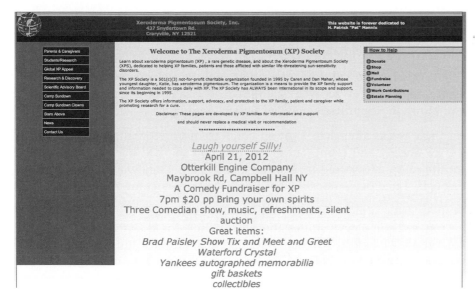

Figure 7.5

The Web site for the XP Society and Camp Sundown.

many parents are hesitant to allow their children to appear on camera. But in this case, these were children with rare diseases and their parents were naturally even more protective. I did not know any of the names of the parents or children who attended Camp Sundown, but I would have to make contact somehow.

I called the number on the Camp Sundown Web site and got an answering machine. I left a message explaining that I was a journalist interested finding out more about the camp and about XP. At this point, I had not yet pitched my story to any publications. I had an idea for a story, but without any sources, I still had no story to pitch. Often, calling from a major media outlet will help you gain access. Most people will return a call from the *New York Times* or CNN. But in my case, I could not yet promise exposure.

A couple of weeks went by and I heard nothing back from the camp. I called again and left a follow-up message that essentially repeated my first message. No call back. A week later, I called again and left another message. A couple weeks after that, I got a call from a woman who said she was involved with the camp. She was a volunteer and the owners of the camp had asked her to speak with me. I immediately called her back. This was my first human contact for this story.

Luanne Meade picked up when I called. Meade was a camp volunteer, and she organizes a night of carnival rides and games for the Sundown campers each year. She seemed skeptical when we spoke. I explained that I was a video producer. I was interested in finding out more about the camp. I wanted to visit the camp, and, if possible, I wanted produce a short documentary about Sundown. I was careful not to make promises about the form of the final project or any potential publishers.

"Well, OK. Let me talk to Caren. Why don't you email me again what you want to do and I can see what she thinks," she said. I hung up thinking that I had blown it. Regardless, I emailed Meade that night.

A couple weeks after that, I got an email from Caren Mahar, the founder of the XP Society and Camp Sundown. She said she had been busy preparing for the camp and would be glad to speak to me. Finally, I had made break-through. It had been months since I first began researching XP.

I called Mahar almost immediately, and it was strange hearing her voice after having read some news stories about her online. I told Caren what I had told Luanne Meade before. We chatted for about 20 minutes and before we got off the phone, I asked, "Can I visit you and Dan? I'm just 2 hours away."

"OK. I can give you directions," she said.

"That's OK. I have GPS." With that, I prepared for my first visit to Camp Sundown.

Camp Sundown is located in a building designed by Dan Mahar on the Mahar's property, just up the hill from their house. It was empty when I arrived. No kids yet. I was greeted by Caren, Dan, and their 21-year-old daughter, Katie, who had been diagnosed with XP when she was 2 years old. We sat in their kitchen for a few hours, chatting about me, my teaching at Columbia, and the Yankees. Katie was a huge fan of Jorge Posada, the

Figure 7.6

Camp Sundown is located in a field behind Caren and Dan Mahar's home.

Yankee's All-Star catcher. We spoke very little about the camp until just before it was time for me to go.

As Caren and Dan gave me a tour of the Camp Sundown building, I finally asked: "Would it be okay if I came to the camp when the campers arrived?"

"I think that would be just fine," said Dan. "But you have to clear it with the parents first." I was making more progress, but I still did not have access to the kids.

The Mahars were the keys to me getting access to the kids and their families. During my visit with them, Caren and Dan had been interviewing me just as much as I had been interviewing them. I suppose I had passed the test. Caren gave me the email addresses of some camp parents. I emailed all of them, and each one agreed to let me interview their kids and to shoot video of them while they were at the camp. And each family told me that Caren and Dan had vouched for me.

It is critical for video journalists to build the trust of sources. In communities or groups that are extremely foreign or provide no easy access, you need to gain the trust of an influential source who can then introduce you to the larger group. An insider advocating for you is invaluable. In my case, Luanne introduced me to Caren and Dan, and Caren introduced me to the mothers. The Mahars' blessing was all I needed.

What you are not producing. Before driving up to Camp Sundown, I made a list of all the things I would need for my week-long stay with the campers and their families. I needed clothes and toiletries, two cameras (in case one

Figure 7.7
Katie Mahar (left) suffers from XP, and was the inspiration to build Camp Sundown.

broke), microphones, lights, batteries, memory cards, a tripod, and a monopod. I wrote down a list of interview questions to ask the kids and their families. I wrote down a list of potential scenes I wanted to capture. Then, finally, I made a list of what I did *not* want this story to become:

- *I did not want this to be a melodramatic sick kids story.* After pre-interviewing the parents on the phone, I realized that, despite having terrifying diseases like XP, these kids lived rich, active lives. It would be easy to produce an emotional story out of footage of sick children, but that would have been too lazy and manipulative.
- *I did not want this to be a story with a convenient and happy ending.* The campers and families at the camp have been living with this disease for years, and they will be living with it well after my story is produced. Their stories don't stop after I am done editing. I wanted to fight the urge to tie up this story neatly. That said, I would still have to find a way to end this piece.
- *I did not want this to be an advocacy piece or fundraising video.* One of the main reasons that the Mahars and the families granted me access to the camp was to bring more attention to the disease and their cause. There are relatively few people suffering from XP, and the disease has been ignored by media, doctors, and drug companies. However, it was not my goal, nor my job, to produce a promotional video for Camp Sundown or the XP Society.

Asking one big question. Once I had gained access to shoot at the camp, conducted pre-interviews, and loaded my gear into my car, I had to figure out the specific story I was trying to tell. There are many *angles* that you can take when researching and reporting a topic. In the case of Camp Sundown, I had a few options:

- *A science and health story.* This angle would explain the disease, the complications it caused, and the treatments.
- *A profile about the Mahars.* This angle would profile Caren and Dan as they fundraised, organized the camp, and worked with the families during the week of the camp.
- *A profile of one of the children with XP.* This angle would not cover the scientific elements of the disease in detail. It would cover his everyday experiences with the disease, and what role the camp would play in his life.

I chose to pursue the third angle. While I would touch upon the science of the disease in my story, I did not want the story to be a clinical video about genetics. I also did not want to profile the Mahars at length. While they do great work for XP sufferers, neither of them suffered from the disease. I wanted to show the experience of children growing up with the disease, in and outside of the camp.

During interviews with the children, their families, and the Mahars, the idea of *normalcy* came up often. Camp Sundown presented an opportunity for the kids to be normal. The children can run around, play baseball, go to carnivals, be around others like themselves, and they never have to explain their condition. I took this theme of normalcy and began to build my story around that.

In my video, I wanted to answer this one big question: *how do you live a normal life when you have a disease that makes everyday activities like going to school, going to the grocery store, or going outside potentially deadly?* The key to producing a focused, visual story with compelling action is to ask a very specific question. To answer my question, I would have to show the ways that my source mitigates the dangers of the sun and UV sources all around.

Finding the protagonist, the conflict, and the resolution. About a dozen XP sufferers and their families attend the camp each year. I could not focus on all of the campers in my story. Too many characters can make your story unwieldy and confusing for the viewer. After days of observing and hanging out with the campers, I decided to focus on a 7-year-old boy named Kevin. Kevin had suffered from UV-related complications his entire life. However, at the camp,

Figure 7.8
Kids at Camp Sundown play outdoors, but only at night.

Figure 7.9
Kids at Camp Sundown celebrate birthdays and holidays together because they are unable to attend celebrations during the rest of the year.

he was outgoing, funny, and, most importantly, he seemed to be unaware of and unaffected by the presence of the camera. Kevin's mother, Jennifer, was also very open to participating in the video.

Relevant action. The camp was a great location for shooting action. There were sports, water slides, night baseball, swimming, camp fires, and talent shows. I shot hours of this footage for a video that would be no longer than 10 minutes. However, I still did not have enough *meaningful* b-roll for my story.

Again, my big question was: *how do you live a normal life when you have a disease that makes everyday activities like going to school, going to the grocery store, or going outside potentially deadly?* I had no b-roll to demonstrate Kevin's normal life away from the camp. I had no footage showing how he and his mother dealt with going to school or going shopping. The b-roll I shot at the camp was well-exposed, well-composed, and full of genuine action, but it was not all the footage I needed to tell my story.

I went to the camp hoping to be able to shoot enough footage to edit as soon as I had returned to my office. I had shot enough material to profile the camp, but that was not the story I wanted to tell. I had to shoot more *relevant* b-roll of Kevin's life at home. I called Kevin's mother, Jennifer, and asked if I could visit them at their home in Virginia. I wanted to spend a few days with the two to see what their everyday lives were like. Jennifer and I had gotten along well while at camp and she quickly agreed to let me shoot them in their home.

Figure 7.10
Even simple tasks such as grocery shopping require Kevin to wear all of his protective gear.

After a 7-hour drive to Virginia, I arrived at their house in time to shoot Kevin putting on his protective lotions, UV wet suit, mask, and visor to go outside. I watched as he went to play in an empty playground in the rain. I shot Jennifer testing UV levels with her meter at the restaurants where they ate. This was the real b-roll and relevant action that I needed to answer my big question. These were the things Kevin and Jennifer did to live normal lives. This footage also gave me the elements I needed to tell a full feature story: the protagonist (Kevin), the conflict (how Kevin must deal with the threat of UV), and the resolution (Jennifer and Kevin have been able to create a normal life with some careful and ingenious workarounds).

Feature story ideas can come from your beat reporting or from curiosities in your everyday life. Regardless of the inspiration for the story, the process of producing these video features will be similar. Feature video storytelling is difficult, time-consuming, and requires you to follow this general process:

- Report and find your story
- Gain access to characters
- Determine what kind of story you do and do not want to produce
- Figure out the one big question to answer
- Shoot relevant action

These steps will increase your chances of shooting enough of the right kind of footage to be able to edit your story in post-production.

Q&A with the Experts: Joshua Davis, Journalist
and Documentary Videomaker

Figure 7.11
Joshua Davis, Journalist and Documentary Videomaker.

How did you get started in video?

I first started working with video professionally in late 1999/early 2000. This was around the time when miniDV and FireWire first came out. It was pretty exciting because, if you were into production back then, it meant you could shoot high-quality video on inexpensive cameras and edit right on your desktop. I lived in Washington, DC at that time, and I found myself working for a lot of nonprofits, and getting modest production gigs with National Geographic and the Discovery Channel.

I really got into video experimenting on my own. In my final semester of undergrad, I decided to make a film. I named it "Tour." My friend's ska band was going on an East Coast tour, and I wanted to document it. So, I spent a month on the road with them, shot some 60 hours of tape, and (4 years later) edited the thing into a feature documentary. The film didn't go far in terms of distribution; however, the lesson learned from the mistakes I made on it help me to this day. And, most of all, the experience taught me how to read a story as it unfolded right in front of my camera.

What kinds of stories work best for video?

The reason I love working with video is because it gives you the unique ability to transport a viewer into the lives of the subjects you are documenting. The bulk of my career has been spent focused on stories about people—character-driven narratives. This type of storytelling really works well with video because it allows you to see, hear, and feel the experiences of others. Video creates a place for audiences to immerse themselves into the lives of subjects, which, when done well, fosters a sense of empathy and understanding for audiences.

What three tips would you give videographers in terms of finding and reporting video-worthy stories?

Know what you're looking for before you approach potential subjects. Like any story, it's critical that you do your background research on the issue on which you are reporting. This will help you focus more closely on what type of character you need to find. Knowledge of the issue will help you to gain that character's trust once you begin reporting.

Get out there and talk to people. Here's a scenario. You're doing your research, you're calling people, but you're making little headway in terms of finding a character. People aren't calling you back. Public relations people are telling you, "No." What do you do? Get out there. Find an event, a rally, a public meeting, a lunch spot—whatever it may be—and just talk to people. The results may surprise you.

Be open and honest with people. If you want your characters to invite you into their lives and open up, you will need to communicate with them well. This means having conversations about your project and why you are doing it—before the camera ever comes out of the bag. Here's an example. I once had a student who had lost access to her subject. She was frustrated, and when she approached her next subject, she hurriedly explained what she "needed" (an interview, access to filming the subject in personal spaces). The subject never really opened up, and it killed her story. When she ultimately found a subject, she did so with a different attitude. She was positive. She engaged her subjects and asked them questions about their lives. She told them why she thought they were interesting and how she could help them share their stories. She later told our class that her greatest takeaway from the project was that she learned that you need to open yourself up to do this type of work. To get to know people and to earn their trust. To share things about your life and be open about your feelings, too. Hearing her say this was one of my proudest moments as a teacher.

How do you get someone to open up to you on camera? How do you get them to "forget" that the camera is there?

The interview is such an important part of the storytelling process because this is where you will find your story. It's in the interview where you discover the conflict, where you go down unexpected roads and find twists and turns in your story that you never imagined. For me, a successful interview starts with making the person feel comfortable. Try and get all your camera and audio ready before they arrive, if you can. Then, just talk a bit. Your goal is for the interview to be more of a conversation.

What are your best three interviewing tricks?

Ask open-ended questions. You will go far with questions that ask how a person felt about a situation. Ask your subject to paint a picture with words about a memory or event. These will often lead to long answers that address entire themes of your interview, not just one specific question. Yes/No questions will get you nowhere.

Deep listening. You want to really listen to what your subject is saying. Follow their story as they express their thoughts and feelings. This will better inform your follow-up questions and help you find the essence of their story. Avoid the chatter in your mind about what the next question in your notebook is or when the camera battery will die. While important, it's even more crucial that you listen.

Limit interruptions. While you want your subject to feel like you are having a conversation, you really are not. It's an interview, and you are actively listening for what your subject is going to say next. Even when they finish a thought, wait a few seconds. They may start up again, and, if they do, it's in this space where I often find the best part of the interview.

When you are in the field, what is in your gear bags?

As a rule of thumb, I like to have a couple camera options (DSLR, GoPro), extra batteries, and some gaffers tape. Here's a list of some essentials:

- DSLR camera
- A few extra batteries
- An audio recorder, a set of wireless lavs, and a shotgun mic with a shoe mount for the camera.
- A few lenses. Preferably one zoom lens (I like a 24–105/f4 or 24–70/f2.8), a low light lens (50/1.2 does the trick), and I LOVE working with a 100 macro for detail shots.
- A lightweight tripod or video monopod
- An intervalometer for timelapses
- Plenty of memory cards
- ND filter
- And a couple protein bars because you never know when you're going to get to eat next.

How do you organize your material in post-production?

Post-production is all about organization. I transcribe all my interviews. I do this in Google Docs because it allows me to easily share these files with other people working on the project. Shared docs also allow for multiple people to annotate and comment on the transcript.

In the edit, I make a sequence for each shoot, and then I place the entire shoot into that sequence. The shots I like, I cut out and pull up to the Video 2 track. Then I duplicate that sequence, rename it so it includes the word "selects," and I delete all the footage I didn't raise to the higher track. It's a pretty efficient way of accessing your best footage, while still being able to go back to your raw clips.

You produce for a lot of organizations. What works best for Web video?
I've always had a love for documentary filmmaking. I got my start working on an independent documentary, and, today, the majority of my work is Web-based documentary. For documentary filmmakers, it used to be that you'd have to work in television to pay the bills. This meant having to produce for a very different style—be it a broadcast news style with narration and time restrictions or (gulp) "reality TV," which is entertainment, not journalism. Now that Web-documentary is pervasive, filmmakers are finding new opportunities to produce documentary video content for newspapers, magazines, and digital publications. The benefit is that the Web created opportunities for filmmakers to experiment with documentary styles while not having to make a feature doc or adhere to television standards.

What advice would you give to new video producers?
One of the best pieces of advice that anyone's ever told me was to be the first to arrive and the last to leave. Do this. Do not underestimate the value of your subject seeing how hard you're working. And you just don't want to miss a good moment. All too often, the best moments happen before or after whatever it is you planned to shoot that day.

CHAPTER 8

Producing a Narrative Documentary

NARRATIVE DOCUMENTARY STRUCTURE

The structure of a narrative documentary is very similar to that of a feature story. Narrative documentaries also include a protagonist, a conflict, and a resolution. But documentaries, by the nature of their length and time of production, also demonstrate another significant element: change over time.

The structure of a narrative documentary is no different to the structure of fiction feature films or television shows with long story arcs. These allow producers to tackle themes and demonstrate character development more in-depth than in breaking news or shorter stories.

Figure 8.1 represents the general structure for a three-act narrative. This form is not specific to documentaries. It can be used for narrative print stories,

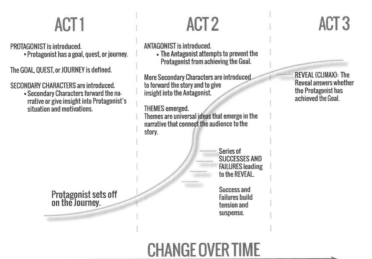

NARRATIVE STRUCTURE IN THREE ACTS

ACT 1

PROTAGONIST is introduced.
• Protagonist has a goal, quest, or journey.

The GOAL, QUEST, or JOURNEY is defined.

SECONDARY CHARACTERS are introduced.
• Secondary Characters forward the narrative or give insight into Protagonist's situation and motivations.

Protagonist sets off on the Journey.

ACT 2

ANTAGONIST is introduced.
• The Antagonist attempts to prevent the Protagonist from achieving the Goal.

More Secondary Characters are introduced to forward the story and to give insight into the Antagonist.

THEMES emerged.
Themes are universal ideas that emerge in the narrative that connect the audience to the story.

Series of SUCCESSES AND FAILURES leading to the REVEAL.

Success and Failures build tension and suspense.

ACT 3

REVEAL (CLIMAX): The Reveal answers whether the Protagonist has achieved the Goal.

CHANGE OVER TIME

Figure 8.1
The structure of a three-act narrative.

novels, or fiction films. The main goals of this narrative structure are to reveal information to the audience throughout the story, to build tension, and to present a complete and satisfying conclusion. Each of the three acts in this structure serves a specific role in achieving these goals.

ACT ONE

The protagonist of the story, the goal of the protagonist, and other relevant sources and background information are presented in the first act of a narrative. During Act One, the storyteller reveals to the viewer what the story is

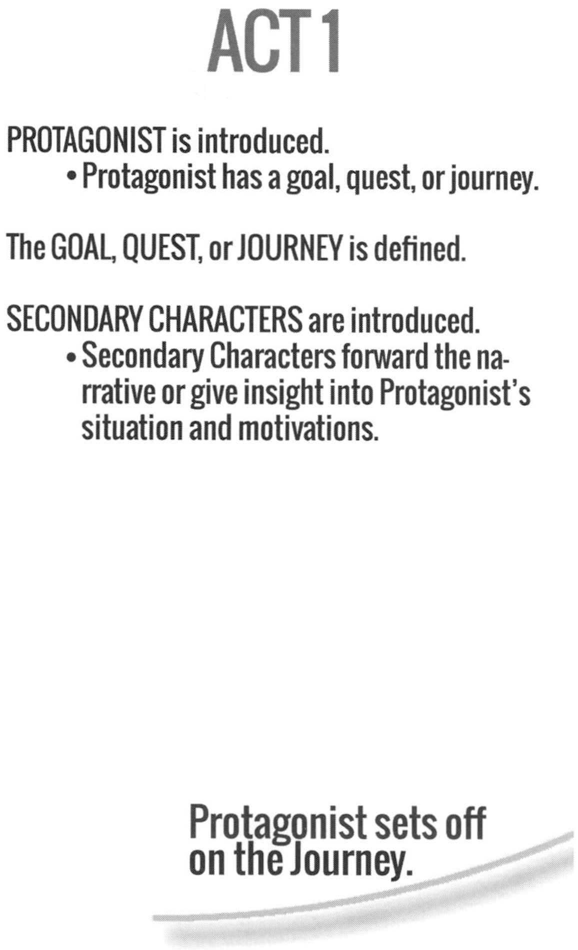

Figure 8.2

The elements of Act One of a three-act narrative.

ACT 1

PROTAGONIST is introduced.
 • Protagonist has a goal, quest, or journey.

The GOAL, QUEST, or JOURNEY is defined.

SECONDARY CHARACTERS are introduced.
 • Secondary Characters forward the narrative or give insight into Protagonist's situation and motivations.

Protagonist sets off on the Journey.

about, who will guide the viewer through the story, and what the audience may learn during the film.

Think about some of your favorite films or novels. In almost all of these stories, the filmmaker or writer declares very early on who the protagonists are, what they want to achieve, and what is at stake for them. In Shakespeare's *Romeo and Juliet*, two lovers from rival families must find a way to be together. In *Star Wars*, Luke Skywalker and the rebels must save the universe from the Evil Empire. In the television series *Game of Thrones*, many characters want to become king and rule the Iron Throne.

While reporting, you may meet and interview many sources for your documentary. But not all characters are protagonists. Some will play other important roles in the film, but it is critical for you to decide who is your main character and what journey he or she will embark on in your story.

- *The protagonist*. The protagonist is the character or group of characters who have a specific goal or quest. While you have many compelling sources, only one will have a clear journey. In fairy tales, knights are protagonists who want to slay dragons and save princesses. In the real world, your protagonist may be a politician running for office, a basketball coach trying to win a championship, or activist trying to raise money for the homeless. A character without a clear and specific goal cannot be the protagonist.
- *The goal or journey*. The goal of the story is directly related to the protagonist. Goals can be large or small, but they are what motivate your characters to act. A musician may need to practice a single song for months to win a spot in an orchestra. An inventor may produce a hundred prototypes before presenting his final product. A restaurant owner must find the best chef. Goals are active processes that can be shot and documented over time.
- *The secondary characters*. Secondary characters give context to the story, provide insight into the protagonist's motivations, or present valuable background information. For example, if you are profiling a politician running for office, his chief of staff or his father may be a strong secondary character. When editing the final version of your documentary, sources who are not protagonists or strong secondary characters must be eliminated.

ACT TWO

Most of the action in the narrative takes place in Act Two. During this act, the protagonist sets out on his quest or journey and attempts to achieve his goal. This is also when the storyteller presents the antagonist of the story, builds

Figure 8.3

The elements of Act Two of a three-act narrative.

ACT 2

ANTAGONIST is introduced.
   • The Antagonist attempts to prevent the Protagonist from achieving the Goal.

More Secondary Characters are introduced to forward the story and to give insight into the Antagonist.

THEMES emerged.
Themes are universal ideas that emerge in the narrative that connect the audience to the story.

Series of SUCCESSES AND FAILURES leading to the REVEAL.

Success and Failures build tension and suspense.

tension, and presents themes or universal ideas to the audience. This is also referred to as the *arc* of the story.

- *Antagonist*. The antagonist is a force that works directly against and deeply challenges the protagonist. The antagonist can be a person, an idea, a policy, or any other element that attempts to prevent the protagonist from achieving his goal. In fairy tales, the antagonist to the knight is the dragon. In non-fiction narratives, the antagonist to a politician may be a rival, the city council, or a lack of campaign funds. The antagonist to a basketball coach may be his inexperience or the lack of skills in his players. Antagonists make the protagonist's journey challenging, a key to building tension in the story.
- *Building tension*. A big challenge for documentary filmmakers, or any long-form storyteller, is to hold the audience's attention to the end of the story. Online, there are many distractions that may draw the viewer's

attention away from your film. Building tension will help to keep the audience's interest.

Building tension in a narrative story requires demonstrating a series of failures and successes on the part of the protagonist. For example, imagine you are profiling a politician during her run for office. Would the story be compelling if the politician had no difficulties or challenges and won by a large margin? Or would the film be more interesting if she had trouble raising money, lost early debates, and if her opponent began a smear campaign? These challenges put the success of the protagonist in doubt. Your protagonist can answer these failures with successful achievements of her own. She may find ways to raise money and win later debates. Demonstrating a series of successes and failures by your protagonist will build tension throughout your story.

- *Themes.* Themes are universal ideas in your story that may be relatable to your audience. Hope, injustice, family, perseverance, and community are some common themes. During Act Two, these themes rise to the surface.

  For example, while your profile about a basketball coach may focus on sports and athletics, the themes that arise may be hope, teamwork, or determination. These themes are universal. Most of your audience may never play in a basketball tournament, but likely they know what it feels like to hope or strive for something. Themes help to make unusual or foreign stories relatable to the audience.

ACT THREE

Act Three is often the shortest part of your narrative. In this act, the results of your protagonist's efforts are revealed. This is when the viewer finds out if your politician has won the race, the activist has been able to raise enough money for the homeless, or the musician has earned a seat in the orchestra. By Act Three, the protagonist has experienced some *change over time.*

ACT 3

Figure 8.4
The elements of Act Three of a three-act narrative.

REVEAL (CLIMAX): The Reveal answers whether the Protagonist has achieved the Goal.

In the theater world, a narrative that ends with the protagonist achieving his goal is called a *comedy*. If the protagonist fails, then the narrative is referred to as a *tragedy*. The quality of the narrative does not depend on whether the story is a comedy or tragedy. Even if the politician loses the election, your story can be extremely compelling and successful. Fans of the Sylvester Stallone film *Rocky* will agree that the film is a classic, even though Rocky loses in the final title bout.

FINDING THE NARRATIVE STRUCTURE IN YOUR STORY

Unlike fiction filmmakers, documentarians cannot fabricate stories. However, you still must craft a compelling narrative from your reporting. This is one of the biggest challenges of non-fiction narrative storytelling. You must determine who your protagonist is, what to use as the goal of your story, and how to end the film. Without a clear narrative structure, the story will become confusing or uninteresting to the viewer.

There are some types of stories that have natural narrative arcs with clear beginnings and ends. Elections, court trials, sports competitions, and calendar years are finite arcs for documentarians to follow and shoot. *Street Fight*, an Academy Award-nominated documentary, detailed Corey Booker's first run for mayor of Newark, NJ. *Heart of the Game* followed a high school basketball team's run at a state championship. *American Teen* documented the lives of teenagers during their senior year of high school. The arcs of these stories were based around a specific event or limited timeframe.

Most non-fiction stories, however, do not have obvious narrative arcs. There will be no election, championship game, or graduation to document. Topics such as poverty, unemployment, healthcare, and HIV/AIDS are not structured around events. This was the problem I faced while shooting and producing *deepsouth*, the award-winning feature documentary directed by Lisa Biagiotti and edited by Joey Lindquist.

CASE STUDY: *DEEPSOUTH*

deepsouth is about the rise of HIV/AIDS in the rural South of the United States. The film is about Josh, a 24-year-old gay man living with HIV in a conservative Mississippi town; Kathie, a fiesty AIDS advocate from Alabama; and Tammy and Monica, two friends who run an underfunded HIV/AIDS nonprofit organization in Louisiana. The film weaves their three stories together, but each storyline follows its own narrative arc.

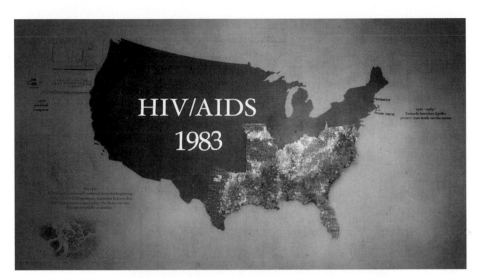

Figure 8.5
*A map from the opening
sequence to* deepsouth.

After months of reporting, Lisa Biagiotti, the film's director, had interviewed nearly 400 sources. Many of these sources gave background information on the science of the disease, the social causes for the rise of HIV/AIDS, and the impact of the disease on these communities. When it came time to shoot the film and to visualize the statistics and data that Lisa had collected, we needed to find and cast the best characters to illustrate this story.

Lisa and I looked for characters who exemplified the experience of living and dealing with HIV/AIDS in the rural South. We wanted sources who were *currently* going through these challenges. We needed opportunities to shoot relevant action and b-roll; interviews could not drive this story. We required characters who were open to spending several days over several months with us. Eventually, we narrowed down the original source list of 400 to our final four protagonists.

Finding the narrative arc. Our next task was to visualize these characters' stories and to craft unique, compelling narrative arcs for Josh, Kathie, Monica, and Tammy. The biggest challenge was that there were no simple or clear endings. There was no election or competition that would neatly finish in a certain amount of time. Long after we stopped shooting, Josh would still have HIV, Kathie would still be driving throughout the country to fundraise, and Tammy and Monica would still be running their non-profit. Their lives and stories would not end just because had we stopped reporting and producing.

Nonetheless, Lisa and I needed to decide on the narrative arc of each story. At one point, we thought of using Lisa as our protagonist. Her goal or journey would be to travel throughout the South to look for reasons for the increase in HIV/AIDS. I would shoot Lisa interviewing doctors, activists, and those infected with the disease. We would document her driving throughout Mississippi, Alabama, and Louisiana until she found the answer. We quickly discarded this concept because it felt disingenuous and too fabricated. We knew that our characters, not a reporter, had to be the protagonists of this story.

For weeks, we debated and discussed potential narrative arcs with Joey Lindquist, the film's editor. We wanted to find simple, demonstrable goals for each character. We wanted each storyline to speak to bigger themes surrounding the rise of HIV/AIDS—hope, family, community, fear, and perseverance—to make this story relatable to the majority of viewers who would not be from the South and who would likely not know of anyone with the disease.

Figure 8.6

Director Lisa Biagiotti, editor Joe Lindquist, and me on location.

Deep into post-production on the film, we decided on the three-act narrative structure for each of our characters. For Josh, we determined that his goal was to find a strong support network. Josh was, by his own admission, alone in his hometown of Greenville, Mississippi. Greenville, deep in the Bible Belt, was a place where many residents refused to acknowledge homosexuality or the presence of HIV/AIDS. Josh wanted to move out, get an education, and build a new life for himself. But to do that, he would need to find a surrogate family and a community to support him.

Gaining access. It took months to get Josh to agree to participate in the film. Off-camera, he was funny, charming, energetic, and insightful—a perfect source for the documentary. But Josh was fearful that the film would bring him unwanted attention. At this point, very few people knew he was gay and that he had HIV.

Lisa, without a camera, made many visits to Mississippi to visit Josh. They spent days talking about his life, driving around the Delta, and exploring abandoned buildings, one of Josh's favorite hobbies. Lisa described the project and the goals of the film. She also clearly explained the ramifications of Josh being on the documentary. He would be clearly outed as gay, not just to his community, but to a global online audience.

Lisa and I had both made many trips to Mississippi before we shot Josh. We had spent a lot of time and money to build a relationship with him, but it eventually reached the point when we needed to get Josh on camera or we would have to move on. Many months after we had first met Josh, he was still hesitant to participate in the film. So, we struck a bargain. We would shoot an

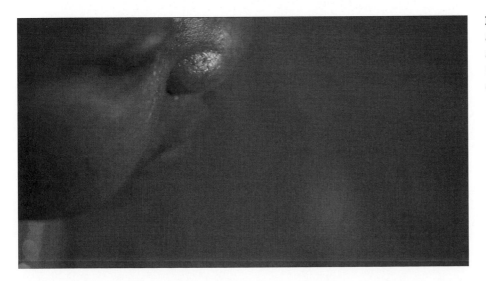

Figure 8.7

Screenshot from a test interview with Josh. This was our technique for concealing his identity.

interview with him, obscuring his face, and then we would edit a short video for his review. If he didn't like how he appeared on camera or what the process felt like, we would not use the interview footage. We would find another source.

Normally, Lisa and I would never make this kind of deal with a source. But asking Josh to be in the film was literally asking him to risk personal harm and injury. We needed to show him we would be honest, discreet, and tactful in our process. After watching the short video (https://vimeo.com/23609574), Josh agreed to be in our film. Ironically, this clip that had convinced Josh to participate in the film never made it into the final documentary. But it was a valuable tool that allowed us to make the movie.

Building the narrative arc. Early in the production process, we had wanted Josh's story to be about fighting the stigma of living with HIV/AIDS in a conservative community, but how could we shoot or show him *fighting the stigma*? This was too intangible a concept to document on camera. We needed to shoot action, not concepts or ideas. How would we illustrate Josh's struggle? How would we show his goal, the antagonists, and the resolution or results of his efforts? There was no obvious beginning or end to his journey. We, the filmmakers, had to build the narrative arc of the story.

We already had Act One. Josh was the protagonist. He was alone and his goal was to find a supportive community. In the first scene of the film, Josh is exploring a decrepit building near where he had been molested as a child. There are no other characters in the scene, and Josh ends up sitting alone in a filthy, abandoned bedroom. This scene was used to illustrate Josh's loneliness and his past. We still needed to find Act Two and Act Three.

Figure 8.8

Cedric enjoying a card game at his home in deepsouth.

As Lisa and I reported and spent time with Josh, we saw that he had found a surrogate father and family 2 hours away in Jackson, Mississippi. Cedric Sturdevant is an AIDS activist who had become a mentor and father figure to Josh and dozens of other young, gay men in the area. Josh often visited Cedric to seek advice and guidance, and we decided that this would be our Act Three. The resolution of Josh's narrative would be that he had been successful in his search for a community. The end of Josh's story, in our film, would be a family cookout at Cedric's house.

Josh's narrative arc was the least literal storyline for us to produce. Act Two, or his journey, would be difficult to visualize. Our other character's stories were more obvious and linear. For Kathie's narrative arc, we chose to show a day-in-the-life of her fundraising efforts. We shot as she went from meeting to meeting. We showed her lobbying government officials unwilling to fund rural HIV/AIDS programs. We shot her writing speeches and growing frustrated, and by the end, we see her exhausted in her hotel room. Tammy and Monica's story arc took place over 72 hours at their annual retreat. Their attendees start out as strangers, but by the end of the weekend, they become close friends.

Josh did not have a time-based narrative, but we needed to shoot his conflicts and successes as he went in search of a new family and support network. For Act Two, we highlight three important scenes: Josh leaving school because he did not have enough financial aid, Cedric telling Josh that he needed to get back to school or he would never escape Greenville, and, finally, the cookout

Figure 8.9
Tammy and Monica singing at church before the start of their retreat.

Figure 8.10

Josh finally finds a family and a sense of home at Cedric's house.

at Cedric's house where Josh transforms from someone shy to someone flirty, from being alone to being surrounded by dozens of friends.

Narrative documentaries can be any length, but most tend to be 30 to 90 minutes long. Sustaining the attention of your audience, especially in an increasingly distracting media world, is one of the biggest challenges for video producers. As mentioned in the *Video Now* report (videonow.towcenter.org), videos online do not have to be short, but shorter ones tend to get more plays. For a viewer to spend 30 or 60 minutes watching a video, that story must entertain and inform the audience until the very end.

Vice News, *Frontline*, and MediaStorm are all companies that have proven that audiences in the millions will watch long-form videos if the stories are carefully crafted with a strong narrative arc: a protagonist, a goal, and a reveal or resolution. Like feature video stories, the inverted pyramid style of storytelling cannot be used for these stories. You must build tension and anticipation in the story, and your audience must wait to find out how it ends.

Q&A with the Experts: Lisa Biagiotti, Journalist/Filmmaker/Director of *deepsouth*

What do you do?

I find myself at the intersection of journalism, filmmaking, impact (government policy/non-profits), transmedia, art, and data/stats/reports (academia).

What makes a story a good video story?

A good video story chronicles experience, documents reality, provides context, and takes the viewer inside a world he/she would likely not have access to. It is

Figure 8.11

Lisa Biagiotti, journalist/filmmaker/director of deepsouth.

more experiential, and less informational. It is layered and rich and often narrow in scope and scene. When you watch it, you imagine yourself in the story. You engage with it on an emotional level, which is much deeper than shedding a manipulated tear.

How do you go about finding characters for your videos?

I'm not sure my process is efficient. I start by combing through all the research and data, interviewing the experts, and then I start talking to people—anyone and everyone. I try to recognize patterns in what people are saying and trends across time and space. I have loose archetypes in my head when I'm in search of characters, based on what I'm reading and hearing. I ask myself: Am I personally interested in this person's story? Do I trust this person? Does this person "stand in" for a lot of other people? How does this person fit into the overarching narrative I'm telling?

This is not a rigid process. I'm also open to surprises. If you have written your story and cast your characters in your apartment somewhere, red alert. You might be missing something or are too set on controlling your version of the narrative. Sometimes you meet a person and they challenge what you planned and you simply must change course. Go with your gut, not your analytic head or your heartstrings.

How do you put sources at ease on camera? How do you build trust so that sources let you go deeply into their lives?

Trust takes time, genuine interest, and respect. I show up (or check in) again and again. I'm responsive. And I listen to what they're saying and not saying. For Josh, the main subject of *deepsouth*, I spent time tagging along in his daily life—driving around the Mississippi Delta, walking around town, watching the sun go down over the levee. Most of this time, we were hanging out and talking—for months. I'm actively listening and trying to understand him, but I'm also watching for the "scenes" of his life as they fit into the story.

I want to emphasize, though, that my source is not my friend. If I were his friend, I wouldn't have told certain parts of his life in the film. His story is in service of the larger story. I explained this to him, and others. I was also honest about what I was thinking, what I was trying to figure out. I asked his opinion on some of my theories. I talked about the other storylines of the film. He became part of the process. Admittedly, it's a delicate balance. My sources are not filmmakers and in the edit bay with us.

What mistakes do you see video producers making? What mistakes do you try to avoid?

The issue is not the story, and video is not print. It is not my job to make a compilation visual report of the reports. For many video producers, the statistic is the takeaway, the *finale*. I don't need to watch a short film of video for you to feed me a statistic. Use each medium to its fullest potential. If print is for information, video is for experience.

I am not trying to impose a storytelling template or copy a cinematic style. I am figuring out what the story is, and going from there. Find the meaning of the data. Translate what you feel and see in a place. Why are you showing what you're showing? What does it mean? I hope it's not filler b-roll, but there is a reason you are pairing the "scenes" of a characters' lives with what they are saying.

How do you find the stories you want to tell? What is your process?

The idea usually stems from something that surprises me—a statistic, the last paragraph of a report, or a side reference to something I didn't know about. They are usually unreported stories hiding in plain sight, or issues that are so tired that we look at them in ways that no longer match reality.

The meaning of the story is hidden in the data point, but that is only my starting point. So when a statistic claims that the rate of HIV infection in the American South is 50 percent higher than the national average, that is NOT the story. It is a catalyst. I set off for some old-fashioned shoe-leather reporting—pen, paper, and rental car keys. In 2½ years, I drove thousands of miles and interviewed hundreds of people to understand the context.

I also could not do this by myself. I surrounded myself with a talented team and constantly bounced ideas off them, trusting their insights and approaches—especially when I'm drowning in a watershed of data and utterly confusing experiences. Don't go at this alone.

deepsouth *was expensive. What advice do you have for new producers in terms of fundraising?*

I can never make another film the same way I made *deepsouth*—where I liquidated my IRAs, moved home with my parents, and lived the life of a gypsy nomad for several years. *deepsouth* cost $97,000 to make, and I was honestly lucky to receive a $50,000 grant from MAC AIDS Fund early on. Now, there are crowdfunding platforms like Kickstarter. These are great options, but know that they take work and commitment.

So before you fundraise and invest in a story, make sure it's a story you must tell. Don't expect any return on your investment. The experience is your pay-off. I often say, if *deepsouth* is the only independent film I make, then I made the film I wanted to make. The end. But because I created something, I have more mainstream opportunities than I had before. I didn't expect this. Expect that no one will care or get it—do it because you can't do anything else.

When you go into post-production and editing, what's your process for finding the story in the hundreds of hours of footage? And how do you shape your ideas into compelling narratives?

We filmed a linear process. How tragic if the story unfolded that way. In post-production, we're structuring the story on emotional and thematic levels. We're trying to maintain consistent (rising/ falling) feelings and a sense of place, assigning meaning to scenes within the overall narrative.

For instance, some of the themes of *deepsouth* are isolation, disconnection, home, and safe spaces. On a surface level, this is a story about poverty and HIV in the rural South. On an emotional level, this is a story about finding home, doing everything yourself to survive, and saying the same thing over and over while no one seems to hear you.

On this plane, we had to figure out which scenes spoke to these overarching themes. Every scene had a meaning embedded in it. When Josh (the protagonist) is running in place for hours, that signifies inertia of his life. It also happens to be something Josh does on a daily basis to get out of his head.

We're distilling the character and story down to meaning, finding universal truths in these narrow portraits. We're transporting viewers into worlds they otherwise don't have permission to access.

What are the three biggest pieces of advice you give to video journalists starting out?

1. Don't wait for people or institutions to give you permission to follow a story.
2. If you do this only once, make sure it's the story you want to tell—with your voice, insight, and perspective.
3. Be a fastidious producer, but learn to let go in the field and allow reality to play out. Trust that life has way more imagination than you do.

CHAPTER 9

Mobile and Smartphone Photography

Any textbook about video production would be incomplete without mention of mobile video. iPhones, iPads, and other smart devices have produced more photos and videos than any other devices in the history of photography. Smartphones are compact, always available, and can produce high-quality sound and images. Most importantly, their connection to the Internet makes it possible for journalists to file breaking news immediately.

Figure 9.1
Shooting video with an iPhone.

WHY MOBILE?

Increasingly, newsrooms are requiring all journalists to use iPhones to report, shoot, edit, and publish video from the field. There are many camera options on the market today, but few have all the features of an iPhone or iPad, the leading smart devices for mobile journalists.

- *Cost*. An iPhone costs less than most cameras, even the cheapest DSLRs. With some data plan agreements, the price of iPhones can drop to a couple hundred dollars.
- *Size*. Smartphones are truly portable. They fit in any pocket and can be used in situations requiring extreme discretion. Even point-and-shoot cameras can be too bulky or attention-grabbing for some reporting environments.
- *All-in-one*. iPhones can be used to shoot, edit, and publish video. Advanced apps can give users more control of their image, audio, and video quality. No other cameras provide full production and editing features.
- *Web connection*. Data plans and Wi-Fi connections make it possible for multimedia journalists to file stories directly from the field. There is no need to return to an office or hotel room to shoot, edit, and upload pictures and video. Additionally, Facebook, Instagram, and Vine are powerful social media platforms where journalists can post news content directly from their phones.

Limitations

- iPhones are not DSLR or video camera replacements. They will not be able to shoot footage as well as a dedicated video camera, and their editing applications cannot realistically compete with the feature set of a full NLE. But once you understand and mitigate their shortcomings, iPhones and iPads can become powerful video newsgathering and distribution tools.
- *Bad audio*. iPhones were designed with microphones for making phone calls, not for collecting high-quality audio. iPhone microphones, like all on-camera microphones, are placed poorly for capturing ambient sound. Additionally, iPhones capture audio using automatic gain control (AGC), limiting the shooter's ability to monitor and adjust audio levels.
- *Fully automatic video*. The iPhone's default video app shoots video on full automatic mode. The shutter speed and ISO are completely determined by the camera's software. There is also no way to control the camera's shooting frame rate or lens aperture.
- *Ergonomics*. The iPhone's most attractive features—its compact size and low weight—are also its biggest drawbacks. The iPhone is too light for steady shooting. You will have to mount some support accessories to the phone to give it enough weight for handheld shooting.

Figure 9.2
Lenses, support brackets, and microphones have all been developed specifically for use with the iPhone.

A huge market of third-party iPhone add-on accessories has emerged in recent years. Lenses, support brackets, lights, and microphones have all been developed specifically for use with the iPhone. Some device manufacturers support Android phones, but because of their uniform design, the majority of third-party hardware and apps have been developed for iOS devices.

Hardware. The iPhone lacks heft and mounting points for attaching microphones and lights. This problem can be resolved by attaching support brackets onto your camera. External microphones should always be used with iPhones or iPads because the built-in microphones have very limited range and are prone to picking up handling noise. Lens adapters can also be added to give your camera wide or telephoto focal lengths.

Software. The best photo, video, and editing apps are available for Apple's iPhone and iPad. Applications such as Filmic Pro give your camera full creative control: manual exposure and audio gain. Editing applications such as iMovie and Videolicious also make editing fast and videos quickly publishable.

Hardware and software for mobile devices are upgraded regularly. Check out duylinhtu.tumblr.com for new product reviews and updates on software applications for producing video on your mobile device.

While hardware and software for iPhones may be updated often, the principles of quality video production do not change for mobile producers. Video

Figure 9.3

Apps such as Filmic Pro allow shooters to manually set focus, exposure, and audio levels.

Figure 9.4

Raw iPhone videos can be uploaded immediately from the field.

stories work best when they demonstrate motion and emotion. You must pay careful attention to crafting well-composed images; the rules that apply to shooting with a proper video camera also apply to shooting on an iPhone. You must also record high-quality audio. And you must remember to shoot scenes with genuine action.

That said, there are some best practices that are specific to using iPhones for mobile reporting:

- *Be fast.* iPhones cannot shoot better images than more expensive cameras, but they are much faster for shooting, editing, and publishing. If you wait hours to publish your videos, then you are drastically minimizing the iPhone's advantage. Publish stories immediately. An iPhone allows you to beat large TV crews to air.
- *Simple edits.* Video editing apps such as iMovie and Videolicious do not have the same feature sets as Adobe Premiere Pro or Final Cut Pro. But they can make quick edits with a couple swipes of your finger. Do not use the same editing technique as you would use on a desktop on your iPhone. Produce your stories with as few edits as possible, and make your edits simple.
- *Raw is good.* Raw video is immediate, requires no editing, and can feel genuine and authentic to viewers. If you have visceral or emotion footage, upload your content, immediately share your video, or embed it into a text story. Raw footage of fires, bad weather, a mile-long traffic jam: a game-winning shot requires no additional video or narration.

CHAPTER 10

Company Profiles

From October 2013 until February 2014, my colleague, Abbey Adkison, and I traveled across the country to visit newsrooms and interview video producers for our *Video Now* report (videonow.towcenter.org). We observed documentary producers, digital-first properties, and traditional print publications that were starting to produce more and more original news video programming. We quickly discovered that each organization had different resources and goals for their video teams. Some newsrooms had two video producers on staff, while others had dozens. Some focused on weekly talk shows; others were committed to producing long-form documentary films.

All of the organizations we visited did have a few things in common. They were all excited about the editorial and revenue potential of video. They were all planning to increase their video output. And they were all still experimenting with online video forms and styles. Despite the decline in print journalism over the past decade, video journalism is in a period of huge growth. Arguably, there has never been a better time for journalists to start producing news videos.

Below are profiles of some of the companies we visited. Each profile details the types of videos they approach, their editorial philosophy, and how they produce their videos. More information about these organizations and other newsrooms can be found at: videonow.towcenter.org.

Publication: *Detroit Free Press*

URL: www.freep.com

Video Team: The *Free Press* video team is led by Kathy Kieliszewski, the Director of Photo and Video. Kathy oversees a staff of 12 photographers and videographers. Shooters at the *Free Press* are required to take stills and produce video stories.

Types of Videos: Since 2006, the *Free Press* has been producing award-winning feature videos. "We want to be the NPR of video," says Kieliszewski.

Figure 10.1
A Detroit Free Press *reporter shoots video.*

Her video team members come from still photography backgrounds, and the videos they produce are cinematic in tone and aesthetics. In 2014, the paper produced its first feature-length documentary, *Packard: The Last Shift* and Kieliszewski launched the Freep Film Festival in Detroit. Along with long-form documentaries, the *Free Press* video team shoots raw video clips, uses video feed services such as Reuters, produces 1- to 3-minute news video packages, and covers major news events such as the International Auto Show.

Freelancers: The *Detroit Free Press* uses freelance videographers, but the majority of their material is produced in-house.

What Works for Them:

"It's been an evolution because we did start out with just doing really high art. We were going to make it beautiful and awesome. You really can't sustain that through multiple projects in a year. You have to be much more selective and surgical about stuff like that. There were days where I was here every single day in a week till four in the morning, and you can't sustain that. I mean, I look back '06, '07, and '08—that was the time we won our four Emmys—I don't think I ever saw my family," says Kathy Kieliszewski.

"In the newspaper, we have lots of different kinds of stories: we have briefs, we have daily news stories, we have enterprise, and then we have really great long-form investigative pieces. We should have all of those things in our video and that's how we've evolved over the course of this 8 years."

Figure 10.2
The Chicago Sun-Times *laid off its entire photography team and built a new videography department.*

Publication: *Chicago Sun-Times*

URL: tv.suntimes.com/

Video Team: Dustin Park, Executive Producer, manages all video operations for the *Sun-Times*. He oversees the production of feature video stories, several weekly shows, and special projects. Dustin also trains and works with print-oriented producers to shoot and produce video on their iPhones.

The *Sun-Times* created a stir in the journalism world when they fired their entire photo department in 2013. Dustin has refitted that team into a Multimedia Production department that features 8 to 10 producers and interns. Members of the multimedia department are required to shoot photos and produce video.

Types of Videos: The *Chicago Sun-Times* produces a mix of programming. Park and his producers shoot and edit long-form documentaries, but they are also responsible for the production of shorter series such as *3 Questions*, Richard Roeper's show, sports programs, and a political talk show that is shot in their offices and features *Sun-Times* columnists and reporters.

Freelancers: The *Chicago Sun-Times* uses freelance photographers and videographers, but the majority of their high-end video packages and shows is produced in-house.

What Works for Them:

"We were just talking about it the other day that in the past 6 months of our metrics, the average view time has dropped 30 seconds. It's gone from 2½ minutes to 2 minutes, and a lot of it is under 2 minutes," says Dustin Park, Executive Producer of Video at the *Chicago Sun-Times*.

"Now, I'm tailoring a lot of our content to work with those numbers. I'm starting to make videos quicker and more bite size. However, I do think there's a huge appetite for documentary video. I feel strongly that there is a space that can be inhabited for documentary video. Whether that's going to be a popular space, that's probably not true. But it never has been true for documentaries. Ninety percent of your business is aimed towards revenue and funding, and, hopefully, you can carve out 10 percent where you can do something that you really care about, regardless of whether or not that's going to make money. I would like to do two, three, four [documentaries] a year. We're trying to do a lot of stuff."

Publication: *Frontline*

URL: www.frontline.org

Video Team: Raney Aronson, Deputy Executive Producer, manages much of the day-to-day business of *Frontline*, PBS's award-winning public affairs documentary series. *Frontline* employs a large network of filmmakers who produce hour-long films for the series. Aronson's in-house team manages the show's digital presence and operations.

Types of Videos: *Frontline* produces 26 to 28 hour-long films a year on topics that range from North Korea to the National Security Agency. For much of its 30-year history, the show has focused its efforts and attention on its

Figure 10.3

Raney Aronson (right), deputy executive producer of Frontline, *watching a rough cut of a film.*

weekly PBS broadcast. Recently, Aronson and Sarah Moughty, head of digital at *Frontline*, have begun to produce and publish digital-first videos exclusively for the Web.

Freelancers: Most of *Frontline*'s films are produced by independent directors and producers with years of experience in reporting and filmmaking.

What Works for Them:

"[Because of the Web,] we feel completely free now to publish things when we editorially think they should be published. When we think it's in the public interest to know about a story, we do not hold it back anymore. We do a ton of collaborations and what I've learned very early working with investigative shops is that we need to publish iteratively. There's no reason for us to hold it back for the broadcast. There's just no reason. What we did instead is we started to publish right away," says Raney Aronson, Deputy Executive Producer.

"We have totally changed our model. We don't think just in terms of how do we get the one-hour. We've transitioned to thinking across platforms now that we can publish right away if we need to. Sarah Moughty [head of digital] is right outside my office. She and I are constantly talking. Our filmmakers are in constant touch, telling us: 'Oh my god, we've got to get a piece of that out.' And then we think really strategically about what part of it we publish early. What do we hold for the film? What do we write about? What video do we publish? It's a constant in-stream conversation that I'm having with the digital team."

Publication: Mashable

URL: www.mashable.com

Video Team: Matt Silverman, Editorial Director, leads a small Mashable video team that consists of two producers and various interns. This team manages video for all of mashable.com, a highly popular news site that focuses on technology and the social Web.

Types of Videos: Mashable produces a wide mix of video content that is published on YouTube, their own proprietary player, and on other networks such as AOL. Their videos range from comedy shows such as *5 Facts* to more serious topics such as 3D gun printing. Mashable also outsources video production to Newsy, a company specializing in fast turnaround of news videos. Silverman's strategy is to combine high-view comedy shows with serious journalism.

Freelancers: Mashable produces most of its video in-house or through third-parties such as Newsy.

Figure 10.4

A Mashable reporter shooting video.

What Works for Them:

"What I have to remind myself all the time is the Internet is so big. There are so many people and there's so much Internet and we can produce stuff and find an audience for it. We produced a beautiful documentary called 'I Printed a 3D Gun' and we continue to see giant spikes on the video. It's got hundreds of thousands of views, which is a great return on a piece of content that we invested a lot of resources in," says Matt Silverman, Editorial Director of Mashable.

"Conversely, we do stuff that's simpler like 'Why Your Facebook Friends Are Annoying.' That stuff is just so compelling to share. We can produce it and cut it maybe in a day or two. Hopefully, it builds audience so that we have the resources and the clout to say: All right, now look at this more sophisticated documentary. In short, there are no rules as far as I'm concerned."

Publication: MediaStorm

URL: www.mediastorm.com

Video Team: MediaStorm was founded by Brian Storm, an innovator in online visual storytelling. Storm manages a team of approximately 10 producers, editors, social media editors, and technology developers. MediaStorm collaborates with independent photographers and videographers to produce long- and short-form documentaries.

Types of Videos: MediaStorm was an early adopter of the audio slideshow format—stories that combined award-winning photography with in-depth

Figure 10.5
Brian Storm (left) of MediaStorm in an edit session.

audio interviews. Their work in this medium was popular and quickly adopted by other news organizations. These days, MediaStorm works primarily in long-form documentary storytelling. Recently, they produced their first feature-length film, *The Long Night*, a collaboration with filmmaker Tim Matsui.

Freelancers: MediaStorm collaborates with independent photographers and videographers. They will also hire shooters and producers to work on various journalistic and commercial projects.

What Works for Them:

"I think we've created a lot of artificial frameworks about how we do what we do as an industry. Why does everything on TV have to be the same duration?" says Brian Storm, founder and owner of MediaStorm.

"Everything's got to be 28 minutes and 25 seconds to leave room for ads. Well, not all stories need to be 28 minutes and 25 seconds. This idea that something should be a set duration, it makes no sense and I think the Web kind of blows that out of the water. Because what you're up against on the Web is people's attention. It's not about duration. It's about quality of experience. It's about keeping them—they're one click away from Facebook. You know what I mean? How do you keep them in a story? Well, a story better be amazing. It better grab them. It better be cinematic and beautiful and better have a narrative that has surprise and apex and structure to it that makes them want to know, 'Is [he] going to make it?'"

Figure 10.6

NPR's highly-successful multimedia project, Planet Money Makes a T-Shirt.

Publication: NPR

URL: www.npr.org

Video Team: NPR has been traditionally known for its radio storytelling. But with the huge success of their multimedia package *Planet Money Makes a T-Shirt*, NPR's new visuals team has already established a reputation for producing innovative, high-quality video journalism. Unlike video teams in most newsrooms, NPR is led by a designer and developer rather than a traditional video producer.

Types of Videos: NPR does not produce a high volume of video. Instead, they spend time working on a select number of in-depth projects. They produce short documentaries that range from 3 to 10 minutes long. NPR's visuals team is comprised of designers, developers, video producers, and editors, and many of their future projects will be integrated Web projects similar to their *T-Shirt* story.

Freelancers: The NPR visuals team is relatively new, and they are working with freelancers to produce much of their video stories.

What Works for Them:

"We don't do a lot of videos because we're not like a daily newspaper in the sense that we have a big video department that can cover all of Washington and big national stories. When we choose to cover something, it's because we think it's interesting enough. We're only going to do like a few videos a year compared to other news organizations that are going to produce that many in an hour," says Ben de la Cruz multimedia editor at NPR.

"Our productions are a little more special in that respect and we treat them that way. We take time to edit because they're usually more evergreen than

Figure 10.7
The Seattle Times *has
a staff of only two video
editors.*

deadline-based news stories. That's one of the criteria. We're not going to do something that's going to be due tomorrow. I think here at NPR they always talk about these driveway moments when you're in your car and you can't leave because the story is going and you just don't want to leave your car. That's what we're striving for with video."

Publication: *The Seattle Times*

URL: www.seattletimes.com

Video Team: Danny Gawlowski is one of only two full-time video editors and producers at *The Seattle Times*. Danny works with photographers and reporters to gather video and to produce video packages. There are no full-time, dedicated video producers currently on Gawlowski's team.

Types of Videos: *The Seattle Times* publishes raw video clips directly from reporters' iPhones. These videos are typically short and low-quality, but fast and immediate. Gawlowski also works on a limited number of long-form multimedia packages such as *Sea Change*, a project that included text, photos, and short- and long-form video stories. *The Seattle Times* also published video stories from their TV broadcast partner.

Freelancers: Gawlowski edits nearly all of the video packages that are produced at *The Seattle Times*. They currently do not use many freelancers for video production work.

What Works for Them:

"We use video in a couple of different ways. We use it to show people's experience. We use it to make emotional connection with our subjects and then we also use it to explain a complex story and help our audience along through it," says Danny Gawlowski, Photo and Video Editor of the *The Seattle Times*.

"When it comes to projects, what I'm trying to do with video is I'm trying to develop an emotional connection with the audience. I think that you can read about the people in a story and I think there are a lot of ways that you can build an emotional attachment. But with video, you can really connect with the subjects of the story, and then you will really understand the issues. The other thing we attempt is to tell incredibly complex stories, like the ones our investigative team tackles. These are really, really complex stories and sometimes I think that video can be used really well to give you a 2-minute explanation so you have a baseline understanding."

Publication: Vice News

URL: news.vice.com

Video Team: Jason Mojica leads a team of dozens of reporters and producers at Vice News. Vice News was launched in 2014 and their team of videographers continues to grow as the company attempts to produce 50 hour-long documentaries per year, as well as a weekly show on HBO.

Types of Videos: Vice News specializes in long-form documentary production about topics ranging from life in North Korea to violence in the Central African Republic. With the launch of Vice News, the organization has begun to focus on shorter, daily video dispatches as well.

Figure 10.8
Vice News has built a large viewership for its video programming.

Freelancers: Vice has an extensive network of freelancers across the globe. While most of their videos are edited in-house, their producer and shooter pool is largely freelance.

What Works for Them:

"I don't think that Vice News intentionally makes things specifically for a younger audience. We've seen people do that particular thing. Generally, some people in a boardroom decide 'We need to make news for these young people. How do we do that? Let's find someone who knows or is down with the streetwise lingo of the young people, and then let's rewrite the news script in this current vernacular.' We don't do that." says Jason Mojica, Editor-in-Chief of Vice News. "We don't try to make things cool or hip or young, but I think there's something about our informal approach that just generates a level of trust even so more than the polished approach of the traditional broadcast journalist, which is meant to imbue professionalism. I think that's what makes our stories so engaging and why people will sit through a long-form documentary."

Index